A Question of Reiki

Beyond the Surface of Energy Healing

Heidi Wirth

Alphecca Books

Copyright © 2022 Heidi Wirth

First published in Great Britain in 2022 by Alphecca Books.

The moral rights of Heidi Wirth to be identified as the author of this work have been asserted.
No part of this book may be reproduced or used in any manner without written permission of Heidi Wirth , except for the use of brief written quotations.

Cover Design by Richard Tucker

ISBN: 978-1-7395936-0-5

ALPHECCA BOOKS

publishing@alpheccabooks.com
www.alpheccabooks.com

Contents

Acknowledgements	i
Part I: Getting to know Reiki	1
1. Introduction	2
2. A Brief Background	7
My Reiki story	10
3. The Basics	13
Myth-busting!	19
Reiki for prosperity / financial abundance	21
"Reiki makes you look younger"	22
4. Reiki – What Is It Good For?	24
5. The Practices Within Reiki	30
The Reiki precepts	31
Reiki symbols	35
Meditations	35
Grounding meditation	37
6. Defining Reiki	40
Reiki is healing	42
Reiki creates the conditions for healing to occur…	45
7. Questions, Questions!	48
8. It's All In The Hands	55
I don't feel anything in my hands – does that mean it isn't working?	56
Exercise: Hatsurei Ho	67
9. The Reiki Trance	69

Part II: Delving deeper — 73

10. A Question Of Healing: Expecting Too Much — 74
- What can we expect with Reiki? — 78
- When to stop doing Reiki — 84

11. Reiki Goes Where It Needs To – So Why The Hand Positions? — 87
- The Reiki hand positions — 88
- Attention! — 90
- To back or not to back! — 92
- The Byosen technique — 93
- Time and position — 95
- 'Reiki is intelligent' — 97

12. Energy Systems: The Tanden And The Chakras — 100
- The Japanese tanden system of energy — 100
- Chakras — 102
- Overactive, under-active, depleted and blocked chakras — 105
- To work with chakras or not — 108

13. Starting With A Strong Base — 110
- Maslow's hierarchy of needs — 112
- Staying centred — 114
- Practices to strengthen your foundation — 115

Part III: Practical Reiki — 118

14. The Nature Of Reiki And Nature Reiki — 119
- The Reiju and the one great Reiki — 119
- Nature Reiki — 123

Animal Reiki	125
15. Depression, Anxiety And Reiki	129
Mind and control	135
Exercise: energy visualisation for re-centering	139
16. Can I Use Reiki For: Weight Issues; Eating Disorders; Stopping Smoking; Drug Or Alcohol Recovery?	140
Identifying the root cause	142
Turning down the volume	143
Emotional self-reliance	144
To talk or not to talk	150
17. Infertility, Pregnancy And Babies	153
Reiki as a complementary therapy	156
Pregnancy	157
Reiki for babies	158
18. Distant Healing	161
Distant healing for the future and the past	166
19. Do The Reiki Symbols Have Power?	170
Reiki symbols	172
The use of symbols today	173
The original meanings of the symbols	174
Here is the interesting thing…	176
Part IV: Practices that complement Reiki	**179**
20. The Psychic Connection	180
21. Seeing Colours, Auras And Energy	190

22. A Question Of Spirit Beings, Reiki And The Shamanic Connection	196
Animal guardians – and the connection with shamanism	199
Angels	202
Reiki guides	205
Spirit beings	206
Exercise: How to connect with angels	209
23. Psychic Attacks And Spirit Intrusions	212
What if I have a spirit intrusion or come under a psychic attack?	220
24. A Question Of Protection	223
Negative energy	224
Emotional feedback	225
Empathy feedback	226
Part V: Beyond personal practice	**231**
25. "Keep It Simple"	232
Trusting your intuition	234
26. You Don't Have To Be Perfect!	237
27. A Healer Has To Have Come Through Trauma To Be A Good Healer (And Why This Isn't True)	242
28. A Little Bit Of Business	247
29. And Finally…	255
Appendix	**261**
Glossary of Terms	262
References	266
Bibliography	268

Acknowledgements

This book has been several years in the making, and it has been a wonderful journey of the two things that I love most: writing, and Reiki. I would like to humbly thank those that have taken the time and energy to help me along the way, and to make this book what it is today.

To Judy W., Martin A., Paul Stephen Reiki Master, your input and feedback was invaluable, thank you so very much. I am honoured to know each of you, and to have had you on-board.

To Val Goff Reiki Master and Holly McCrossen of Holly McCrossen Counselling (Norwich), your expertise and help with some of these chapters was gratefully received, with much appreciation.
To my family, who offer me encouragement in all things, and most importantly, love.

To my five year old self who always dreamed of writing a book, thanks kid.

For Liz Miles, Mum.
With love unending.

And for Richard,
My partner in Reiki, in love, and in all things.
Thank you. I love you.

Part I: Getting to know Reiki

1. Introduction

"It is believed by experienced doctors that the heat which oozes out of the hand, on being applied to the sick, is highly salutary ... It has often appeared, while I have been soothing my patients, as if there was a singular property in my hands to pull and draw away from the affected parts aches and diverse impurities ... Thus it is known to some of the learned that health may be implanted in the sick by certain gestures, and by contact, as some diseases may be communicated from one to another."

- *Hippocrates*

Reiki is becoming increasingly popular as a self-help, well-being energy healing modality. Yet, because of its ephemeral nature, it still finds itself on the edges of even complementary therapies. Everyone seems to know someone who does Reiki, and at the same time Reiki is seen by many as a vague, undefined practice and treatment. What exactly is Reiki? What do we mean when we say that Reiki is "energy healing"? How does it work? Why does it work? How can it help me? What are its effects?

Reiki is, quite simply put, an energy-based healing method to help heal ourselves and others. This description sounds a bit hazy and may be puzzling for those who want a clear and precise definition of how it works and what it does. No wonder then that Reiki struggles to find acceptance and be valued in the wider community. It doesn't sit contentedly in people's minds alongside any other type of therapy, yet it happily lends itself to many strands. Reiki isn't massage; there is no manipulation of the body. It's like meditation, but is more than this. It isn't yoga or tai chi; there is no movement required. And it's certainly not a medical or conventional therapy or treatment. It can – and is – used alongside all of these, however, to improve mental, emotional and physical well-being.

Anyone who has had a Reiki session or taken a training course will have experienced the benefits that it can bring, from the inside out, in body, mind and spirit. I am passionate about Reiki as a healing treatment, as I have seen and felt first-hand how it can help oneself and others in a simple and gentle way.

Whether you are new to Reiki and are curious, or you are about to embark on your Reiki journey, or even if you have completed your training but still have questions, this book seeks to show you how simple yet multi-faceted Reiki is, exploring the deeper layers of this practice, and to give an alternative description than just "energy-based healing". We will discover what Reiki can bring to each of us, from all backgrounds and belief systems, and how it sits comfortably alongside medical conditions and treatments, as well as alternative or complementary therapies of all types, and through to more esoteric aspects of healing, spirituality and beliefs.

Reiki is such an interesting modality because it can be both practical and spiritual, and even esoteric. It's practical because it's simple and easy to learn. It requires nothing from us except to understand and connect with an underlying energy that is within all of us, and to put our hands on ourselves or others to let that energy flow. In this way, we can aid physical as well as mental and emotional healing, bringing a sense of inner calm and peace. It's also spiritual because as we practise Reiki we may begin to open

Introduction

our minds and hearts further, connecting on a deeper level to ourselves, to others and to all that is.

Through hands-on healing and meditation practices, the system of Reiki can increase our own sense of spirituality, whatever that means for us as an individual. It can also, if we are so inclined, help with the development of psychic abilities. Reiki doesn't require any proscribed set of beliefs, but can be accessed by all of us, whatever our background and belief system. Each of us can take from it what is right for us, both as a healer and as a receiver of the healing.

This book isn't intended to be a how-to guide or a walk-through of Reiki: there are already many excellent books that address this. I do go through the basics in the first chapters, for anyone coming to this subject for the first time. This book is an attempt to answer the many questions that arise about Reiki in our current times. A lot of information has blossomed on social media, creating a wealth of questions, confusion and some misunderstandings. I hope to answer those questions, and to provide you with a framework to understand the depth of the practice, blowing away the myths and misunderstandings that have cropped up around it.

Students of Reiki – and those who are just curious – come from all walks of life, with a variety of belief systems, expectations and assumptions, so they may all take a different view of the information on social media. Teachers and practitioners of Reiki also come from a wide variety of backgrounds; someone who has trained with one teacher may get a different experience or understanding of Reiki than someone who has trained with a different teacher. A one- or two-day workshop can't impart all of the knowledge and understanding that a teacher has picked up in their years of training, so, even if you have been on a course, you may still have some questions.

Today, many other ideas and practices have become incorporated with and around the simple hands-on healing of Reiki, such as crystals, angels and spirit guides. People often ask whether you should have knowledge of these to be able to do Reiki. On the other side of the spectrum, people ask if Reiki can help with physical issues and habits, such as chronic conditions, addiction or trauma.

How can you be a more effective healer? How do you know if you are doing Reiki right – or wrong? What if you don't feel anything when doing self-Reiki or giving a treatment to someone else? What if you have taken a course in Reiki and are overwhelmed by all the information from it? Or perhaps there wasn't enough information and you have seen things in books or on social media that weren't covered in your course? What about psychic attacks and cutting energetic cords? What if you don't believe in that esoteric stuff, but you like Reiki? What if you do believe in the esoteric stuff, but don't know where to start?

Social media can be a wonderful mechanism for supporting a community that otherwise might feel rather alone geographically; it allows us to come together and support one another, sharing ideas and experiences. It's a great tool for getting information out into a wide public space, but sometimes that information can be too abbreviated and condensed, and therefore it can be misconstrued.

People who are new to a skill – in this case, Reiki – seem to feel that they have to know everything within months or even weeks. This simply isn't true, and it can't be done. Not really, not truly, not for that real, deep understanding that is earned through experience. It's a bit like the difference between a map and the actual terrain: a map shows you what to expect, but you don't experience the mountains, the rivers or the expanse of the land just by looking at a map! The same is true with questions on Reiki via social media … It creates the map, but you can only know the terrain through actually experiencing it.

The potential issue with asking questions about Reiki on social media is that responses tend to be brief and everyone has a different opinion.

Introduction

Some comments and posts can come across as very rigid, with statements such as: "You must and should connect with your guardian angel" or "It will come with Reiki level two" or "You have to have your hands in exactly this position and in this order". This may be helpful for some people, but as universal statements, these simply aren't true. This, as well as the shorthand memes, create something on social media that is at odds with the truth of the practice; the slow, patient, ongoing self-development work. This is a shame for those starting on their Reiki journey: you shouldn't feel as though everything has to happen right now, or that you are doing it wrong if you are not doing things the way that others say they are doing them. Everyone is different, and the experiences that we have are different.

There is no comparison or competition within Reiki practice. First and foremost, the system of Reiki is to help with the development of one's own well-being. It's enhancing our own self-understanding, peace of mind and holistic health. However you wish to experience Reiki, you don't need to worry about anything: at its heart, at its very foundation, Reiki is a simple and gentle healing modality.

This book isn't intended to be a replacement for taking a course or workshop in Reiki – indeed, it can't replace the teachings from a course or perform the attunement, known as a *Reiju*, which is the method through which a student opens up to their own Reiki with the help of their master teacher. This book is a companion, a guide, for anyone who is interested in learning more.

2. A Brief Background

> "First the mind must be healed
> Second the body must be made sound
> If the mind is healthy, conforming to a path of integrity
> Then the body becomes sturdy of its own accord."

- Mikao Usui

Reiki came to us originally from Japan, founded by Mikao Usui, in the 1920s. Usui Sensei (Sensei means "teacher") was a Buddhist priest, so the origins of Reiki come from a background of Buddhism and possibly Shinto, both of which were the prevalent beliefs of Japan at that time. The full history of Reiki is given in many other books and is worth researching if you are interested. To give a brief overview, Mikao Usui found Reiki as a healing method after conducting a mountain meditation as part of his own spiritual practice. He didn't coin the term Reiki, which was already a concept in use in Japan, but he did create the structured system that we know today. Having discovered this way of healing and the spiritual understanding that came from his mountain retreat, he refined the system in order to teach others. Over time, Usui Sensei taught the system of Reiki to around two thousand students, only eleven of whom received the master teacher training.

Usui travelled around Japan to teach, and met a retired naval officer, Chujiro Hayashi, who later received the master training. Usui died in 1926, and Hayashi continued to help heal others and to teach Reiki. He opened a Reiki clinic in Tokyo, where a lady named Hawayo Takata came for healing. Originally from Hawaii, she eventually learned Reiki from Hayashi Sensei. Takata returned to the US and started to teach this system of healing to others. She felt that Americans at that time wouldn't understand Reiki in its traditional Japanese form, so she adapted it for her own students. Those students then added their own understandings and beliefs to the system, and these adaptations carried on down through each student generation. It's from here that Reiki spread across to Europe.

There are now different branches of Reiki as teachers have created their own system, such as Angel Reiki, Tera Mai, Seichem, and many others. Each branch teaches Reiki in a slightly different way, although the foundation of energy healing is the same.

Western cultures have no traditional understanding of *ki*, a subtle energy system that underpins physical health and well-being. The existence of such an energy system is the fundamental principle in many Eastern traditions, including in martial arts forms, spiritual practices and Reiki.

In Japan, subtle energy is part of the cultural heritage; the idea is simply there – it's not "other"; it isn't exotic or strange. However, we in the West need to overcome our cultural conditioning to accept these ideas. We need to work that little bit harder to gain a full and true understanding of integrating *ki* as part and parcel of a holistic self and part of the natural world around us.

The evolution of Reiki in the West to make it understood more easily by an entirely different culture has created some misunderstanding around how and why Reiki works. This idea of an underlying energy that runs through all things has today become almost like some kind of magic, and it's perceived as something mysterious and separate to everything else – whereas really, we should realise that it's pervasive in all things.

Our understanding of *ki* is naturally quite different to the way in which it is understood in the East; the idea of health and being healthy is based on the free flow of one's inner energy, such as in the practice of acupuncture. This cultural difference naturally affects the way that we perceive Reiki, and indeed, other forms of inner energy work such as tai chi, qi gong and yoga. These forms have spent years promoting the understanding that they are about more than just the mechanics of the practice – the physical doing of them – and to realise that it's the *inner work* that is key.

The *ki* in "Rei-**ki**" is the same as *chi*, *qi*, and *gi*; *ki* is Japanese; *chi* and *qi* are Chinese, and *gi* is Korean. These represent underlying energy, subtle energy or spiritual energy. Yet "**Reiki**" is the "universal" energy, or the underlying energy that is all around us, everywhere, rather than just our own energy within us. It's perhaps worth stating here that when we call Reiki "energy", we are not talking about energy in scientific terms; we are talking about an *essence*. Something that exists but isn't directly measurable. Reiki healing really needs to be experienced to be understood.

"Spiritual energy" is the closest term we can use to understand something so naturally ephemeral. Yet there is no *transmission* of energy with Reiki: it's a practice that helps us to balance and align all that is within us to enable healing to take place on any and every level. If we perform a Reiki healing for others, we are creating a space to allow healing to occur, or to allow that person to come into balance and alignment within themselves. We are not transmitting energy; nothing happens except *being – being open*, in a state akin to meditation. No time; no thoughts … just awareness. You can think of this like entering a state of *meditation plus intention*. In that space there is connection, and within that connection, healing can take place.

A healer or practitioner doesn't *give* energy to another, but rather holds open mind, heart and being for Reiki, universal essence, to flow, to be accessed, allowing the person to receive the healing that they need. I hope that reading further in this book begins to make this concept clearer, and that your understanding of Reiki will increase – but there really is no substitute for the experience of a healing session or in taking a course. Calling Reiki "energy" is a shortcut to understanding something that is so intangible.

My Reiki story

I discovered Reiki in 2004, when I was in my mid-twenties. I knew nothing at all about Reiki when I came across it, but I was at a stage in my life where I felt lost, and that my outer life – my behaviour and my job – didn't match how I felt inside. I was looking for a purpose and for something meaningful. I always had an interest in spirituality, but I had fallen into bad habits and didn't know how to change them. By chance, a friend of mine happened to mention that he knew a lady who was running a course on Reiki, a healing energy modality. Out of curiosity, I went along to meet her. On that first meeting, on impulse, I decided to do the course. That lady was Jan de Avalon, my first master teacher, and I remain ever thankful to her for her teachings.

I had no idea what I was letting myself in for, or what to expect, but I was willing to take that chance. I didn't regret it: I immediately fell in love with Reiki and felt like I was drifting on cloud nine for a week after the course! I felt so different; lighter, clearer, my mind empty of the heaviness and clutter it usually had stored in there. I couldn't wait to find out everything about it, so I spent the next ten years doing Reiki for myself and my friends and family.

I read about it and read around it. I continued to develop my understanding of all that it encompassed, and that understanding continually changed as I delved further into the practice, reading more and through my own experiences. Reiki helped to change me – or helped me to change myself – in so many positive ways. I began to understand myself more, at my "inner" core, and to connect with it rather than with my surface emotions of anger, hurt and shame. Gradually I learnt how to move through these, to look at them and to release their hold on me. I learnt why and how I need not take events and others' actions so personally, and to be able to let go of things. I became more gentle with myself.

There are so many ways in which Reiki has affected my life, but I think the biggest change, the most profound, was the blossoming of self-love, self-forgiveness and compassion. That was a real life-changing personal lesson for me, and I believe for many other people too who find their way with Reiki. It also helped me to bring out my inner sense of spirituality; to find the true path with my personal identity, to understand what spirituality meant to me, and the strength that I have found through that.

I knew after my training that I wanted to work with this wonderful, beneficial healing energy full time, professionally, but it seemed such a big step to take, and a scary one. After ten years, during which time I had changed jobs several times and had a family, I was finally pushed into setting up my own Reiki practice by what one could term a cosmic kick in the butt.

At the time, I was working in an office job that didn't fill me with purpose, that was the same day in and day out, that held no creativity. I was stressed with finances and being a mum as well as holding an unfulfilling job. Eventually, I ended up sick with depression and anxiety. It took a while for me to get it, but finally I realised that I couldn't go back to my job and keep my mental health. It was at this point that I knew I had to take the risk and set up my own Reiki business. I haven't looked back since, and I love what I do. I love teaching, helping people find their own path with Reiki, and I love helping clients and seeing their healing journey.

I originally trained in Usui Shiki Ryoho Reiki (sometimes called "Western" Reiki). I have also more recently trained in Jikiden Reiki Shoden (level one). Western Usui Shiki Ryoho Reiki is an original branch of Reiki as taught by Mrs Hawayo Takata, and Jikiden Reiki is Japanese Reiki – it's a system of Reiki that stayed in Japan and is therefore (probably) closer to the original teachings than any Western branch. As I discovered more about Reiki and its many different branches, I never felt a need to seek out the other forms, as Usui Reiki felt right for me, and I liked that it was close, or as close as any Western Reiki, to the original teachings. I appreciated, and still do, the roots and origins of Reiki (although there have been many changes to each named branch of Reiki, so there is no one "original" or "true" teaching). When I heard about Jikiden Reiki, I was intrigued and felt that this would be a good branch to learn because of its cultural ties to the origins of Usui's teachings. In 2019, I finally had the chance to learn Jikiden through a new friend, Paul Stephen, who himself had undertaken his training with Frank Arjava Petter, author of several Reiki books including The Original Reiki Handbook of Dr Mikao Usui. I remain thankful to Paul for this opportunity that has further deepened my understanding of the roots and foundation of Reiki.

There are many reasons why people come to Reiki, for training or for healing sessions, and each person will feel about it and take from it what is right for them – each of us will walk our own path with it.

Reiki is great for helping us to find ourselves, and to feel balanced and whole, in a world that may feel stressful or like it's losing its lustre. Some people come because they want a way to heal themselves or a friend or family member from a physical or mental health condition, alongside conventional treatments; yet others come to Reiki simply out of curiosity.

One of the things I love about Reiki is that it can feel like an answer to something we are searching for: it's a tool for health and well-being, and because of its simplicity, it's something that we can do for ourselves. It's inclusive – anyone and everyone can benefit from the system, practice and gentle healing, and absolutely anyone can learn Reiki.

3. The Basics

"We humans hold the Great Reiki that fills the Great Universe. The higher we raise the vibration of our own being, the stronger the Reiki we have inside will be."

- A note from a student on Mikao Usui's teachings

As a Japanese word, "Reiki" translates into English as *universal life force energy* or *spiritual energy*. It's the essence of all that is, of the (non-physical) energy that runs through every living thing. When we connect with this universal energy, we can engage healing to occur from within – that is, as we heal ourselves through balancing our own inner energy, we can heal every part of us – our mind, our emotions, our physical self.

The *ki* of Rei*ki*, the *ki* energy, is also the equivalent of the word *prana* from India. *Prana* translates as breath; however, that breath is also energy – they are one and the same. Our breath is our energy; our energy is our breath. If we take this word *prana*, then we can also interpret Reiki to mean the *divine breath of the universe*. This translation is a personal favourite of mine!

For Usui Sensei, the practice of Reiki was a path toward spiritual growth. It was a way to help people to develop the:

The Basics

"improvement of body and mind"
- Mikao Usui

For those who may be unfamiliar, let us take a quick look at the basics of Reiki.

- Reiki is a hands-on, or just off the body, energy-healing practice.
- It can be performed for people, animals and plants.
- We can practise the hands-on healing for ourselves and for others.
- It's safe for everyone – in pregnancy, and for babies, children, adults and older people.
- It's safe to use for all conditions and all circumstances, including mild one-off conditions (cuts, bumps, headaches, stomach aches), pre- and post-operations, medical conditions such as arthritis, fibromyalgia and chronic fatigue syndrome, addiction recovery, trauma healing and end of life care.
- Reiki can be used as a regular practice, just like meditation, to help us maintain inner strength, peace and well-being.
- It's safe alongside any medicines, and any other complementary therapy.
- Reiki can help to balance our chakras (energy centres).
- Reiki isn't religious, although it comes from Japan, with Buddhist and possibly Shinto roots. Reiki can be incorporated into any religious belief system, or none.
- The system of Reiki includes the *Reiju* (attunement), which is performed by a Reiki master for the student to open up to their own sense of Reiki.
- As well as hands-on healing, it also includes meditations, precepts and the use of specific symbols (more about these can be found in chapter 5).
- Reiki can help our personal spiritual growth and development.

What does spiritual growth mean? This is subjective because it will mean something different to each one of us. I use it here to mean personal growth: growing through healing, growing in our personal development, and becoming more aware of our innermost self.

Reiki is a wonderful healing tool because of its very simplicity, and it has no contraindications or side effects. Nor is it a talking therapy – it can be, but a person doesn't need to dredge up all their emotional issues or trauma to gain the benefit from a healing session. They can simply relax and allow the practitioner to perform Reiki, experiencing whichever sensations and feelings come up for them.

The usual sensations felt during a Reiki session include heat or cold in the area where the practitioner's hands are, tingling or pulsing in the body, waves of energy flowing through the body, seeing colours or even visions, and sometimes physical sensations such as sudden aches or movement, or feeling a shifting going on. These are normally accompanied by a feeling of peace or relaxation, although sometimes people have an emotional response to the treatment and may feel like crying or find they are restless. This is often ascribed to the re-balancing of the energy, which can clear feelings or stored emotions that are no longer needed and are being released. The benefits for each person are varied, changing with each individual, dependent upon the person's own needs at that time.

At the very foundation, most people find a Reiki session incredibly relaxing. Their thoughts calm down and their minds lose the busyness of the chitter-chatter, feel more grounded and in their body (as opposed to being in the mind), and feel better in themselves physically and emotionally. After the first session, many people get what I call the "rabbit in headlights" look: because Reiki is so different to anything else in our society, people are often aware that something has happened, and that they feel different, but they can't process it – they can't verbalise it. It can take a few hours or even days after that first session for someone to understand how they feel and recognise the benefits of the session. Reiki is accumulative, so continuing sessions can see deeper layers of healing emerge, with an expanding awareness and a sense of calm and clarity. One session of Reiki isn't going to magically fix everything, but it can help us to become more in line with our "inner self", to shake out the stress and tension that has been building up for a while.

Reiki can be practised regularly, and not just when something is wrong: it helps us to maintain balance, to keep healthy and open in mind and body, and to minimise physical, mental and emotional disturbances before they arise. It can also help to increase our sense of compassion, both for ourselves and towards others, and help us in our personal growth and development. In other words, to become a better version of "our self", to become more aligned with our "inner self".

"The deepest level of healing for ourselves is ... to rediscover our True Self, and the deepest level of healing others is to help them to rediscover their True Self."
(Stiene, 2015)

Rediscovering our true self means to be who we are in our inner core, bringing this out into the light, aligning this with our outer self. It means to be able to go beyond our surface emotions and reactions, to be our more aware, peaceful and understanding self.

A full healing session is usually performed with the client or recipient lying down, for anywhere between 30 and 90 minutes. It can also be done seated, and shorter sessions can sometimes be just as effective. The practitioner or healer places their hands at certain points on the body, from the head all the way down to the feet, covering all areas of the body, the major organs and the major energy centres. However, if someone has a specific issue, the healer can place their hands just on the areas that need healing. Reiki is intuitive, and the healer will be guided to where they feel the client or recipient needs healing at that time, in that session.

Despite the wonderful benefits of Reiki, it isn't a magic cure or a quick fix, and this is one of the aspects that I address throughout this book. It isn't going to magically heal, cure or fix someone of a condition or illness in one session, or two, or even fifty … It may help to mitigate and minimise some symptoms, but it isn't a cure-all!

For those who have taken a course in Reiki, it can indeed feel like magic; to have the ability to help heal oneself and others from the inside out feels like a miracle! Miracles can occur – the sudden and immediate shifting or clearing of a physical or serious emotional condition – but they are just that: miracles. The sudden "fixing" of something that is wrong doesn't happen every day, every time.

To really understand the depth of Reiki, there are no shortcuts. We must continue our practice, and continue to develop and learn, just as with any other skill in life. It can take time, and it's okay to not have all the answers within days, weeks or months of learning Reiki. I have been practising for over sixteen years, and I am still learning. Through my ongoing practice of meditation, hands-on healing and focus, I understand myself at a deeper level and am able to explore my emotions and my mind, and to recognise the patterns of my own energy cycles.

In Usui Reiki and Jikiden, there are three levels of training:

- Beginner – level one – *Shoden*. Focus on the background of Reiki, its history, the lineage, the Reiki precepts, and practical application for self-healing and for family and friends.
- Advanced – level two – *Okuden*. For those who want to develop further with Reiki, for personal and professional development. This is now the professional practitioner qualification. *Okuden* focuses on the Reiki symbols, mantras and distant healing.
- Master level – *Shinpiden*. This is sometimes split into Master and then Master Teacher, as this level teaches the *Reiju*, and allows a

student to begin teaching Reiki classes. You can complete this course for your own personal and spiritual development.

The other branches have their own levels of training, sometimes going well above level three. Each branch sets the framework for Reiki training in its own way.

Going to a local teacher to learn Reiki is the best way, if possible. There are now companies that offer online courses. However, these only give distant attunements, which most insurance companies and Reiki associations don't recognise, so you would need to retake a Reiki class in person if you wanted to go into professional practice at any point in the future. In-person classes also offer you the chance to give and receive Reiki treatments with the other students, which is obviously a great foundation to build your knowledge and confidence. Online courses are good for anyone who feels that an in-person class would be a struggle for them, or if they don't have a local teacher.

It's recommended that you leave a gap between each training level of Reiki, spending at least three months practising on yourself, and friends and family if you and they are willing, to get to know and appreciate its feel and effects. This allows you to fully integrate the knowledge, so that you are then wholly prepared for the information at the next level.

For Usui Reiki, the recommendation is that you take the master level no less than nine months after your level one course. This is a suggestion only, though. Some students feel ready to move through the training more quickly than this, while others are happy to wait for years before moving to level two or master. It's fine to not want to take the next level and to learn just for yourself at level one, or to take level two for personal development only.

After your first Reiki course, it may be worth keeping a Reiki diary, writing what you experience during each self-Reiki session and what you notice in yourself in the following days and even weeks. Looking back at this diary after a number of weeks or months may give an interesting insight into what impact Reiki has had on your mind and body.

Sometimes you may feel Reiki turning on by itself: new students, after the first attunement and level one training, often feel their hands heating up of their own accord, even when they are not engaged in Reiki in any way. You may be sitting watching TV, or chatting with friends, and become aware that your hands feel extremely hot and may be buzzing. This seems to be a reaction to the attunement, the awakening of the energy within, and is perfectly normal. If this happens, simply place your hands on yourself, or someone else if you are with them and they are willing, and just let Reiki flow. This will help to calm the heat and energy.

Myth-busting!

Despite all of the excellent information out there through books, classes, talks, online tutorials and on the internet, there are still some persistent myths regarding Reiki. Here are some of the common ones.

- Any type of metal in the body affects Reiki, from metal plates to piercings.
- Reiki will affect a pacemaker.
- The Reiki symbol *Cho Ku Rei* can increase a tumour.

Reiki helps to balance and align our own energy, bringing us to a place of calm and well-being from the inside out. *Reiki can do no harm!*

None of the above myths are true; they come from decades ago when the origins of Reiki weren't so well known and the practice was misunderstood. Metal in or on the body – piercings or a metal plate, for example – won't affect or be effected by Reiki. There is no evidence of this, nor that Reiki affects, or has ever affected, a pacemaker. As for the Reiki symbol – well, can any symbol that we use, such as the Christian cross, the Yin-Yang, and so on, affect a tumour? These don't, and it has never happened. Further information on *Cho Ku Rei* can be found in chapter 19.

Reiki will never, *never* cause cancer to get worse! There are many voluntary organisations using Reiki as one of their therapeutic treatments for cancer patients and their families. It's also used in hospices and hospitals, and there is no evidence of harm for cancer patients. A number of studies have been conducted which show that Reiki is effective in improving the mental health of cancer patients:

"Observational studies have evaluated such integration: In 118 patients undergoing chemotherapy, the 22 patients who received four Reiki sessions had significant reductions in anxiety and pain ... first-time Reiki sessions in 213 patients with cancer indicated that self-reported distress, anxiety, depression, pain, and fatigue each decreased by more than 50%."
(Fleisher *et al.*, 2014)

Another study states that:

"The differences shown between and within subjects suggest that Reiki intervention in breast cancer patients the day before the surgical procedure is an effective practice in improving the general patients' wellbeing."
(Chirico *et al.*, 2017)

While this is good news, we must be aware that the studies are limited, due mainly to the fact that not much funding has been put forward to study Reiki. Some of the published studies do show some improvement in anxiety and pain levels, and not one mentions any harmful effects from Reiki.

Reiki brings mind and body into balance: we don't *give* anything when in Reiki, we don't *take* anything, and we don't *transmit* anything. We connect with the essence, the *ki/chi/qi* that is already there, everywhere. How could the divine breath, the *universal ki*, that simply is, have a malignant effect on cancer or any other health condition?

Reiki for prosperity / financial abundance

This is something that I come across quite often on social media – people asking for Reiki to help with finances or to bring prosperity. I even see Reiki practitioners and healers posting "sending Reiki to increase financial abundance – just type yes!"

This makes me feel quite uncomfortable. How do we think Reiki is going to bring more money to us? What is the mechanism by which this could happen? Reiki isn't a magic lamp; it isn't a wish granter! It's simply a healing method. Materialistic desires and gains had no part in the original teaching.

If we practise Reiki or have sessions from others, we know that it's all about bringing balance and harmony and self-development. It may help us to heal from physical wounds, emotional stress, trauma or past issues. What then does this have to do with prosperity and abundance? If you are wanting to "manifest desires", whether financial gain or another material desire, that isn't Reiki – that is something else.

If we are in a difficult financial situation and need some assistance, Reiki may help at the root cause of our issue. As an example, it may help us stabilise the emotional impact of our circumstances and think clearly and calmly. It helps us to see the problem from a new angle, be able to consider all available options, and understand which one to choose to be able to move forward. The effect of the healing may be to allow us to let go of attachments and judgements. In letting go of attachments, we can find acceptance of our situation and the choices in front of us. Not every situation is an easy one, but there can be a peace that comes when we accept what is, rather than what we would wish to be.

Taking this example further, on a slightly more esoteric level, it may be that Reiki helps to align our energetic or spiritual self so that synchronicities occur that enable us to change our fortunes, or to see opportunities that come our way that may not have been there before. Opportunities that may lead us to a better job, a new friend who can help us, or a house in just the area that we were looking for. I can't deny the concept of such synchronicities, as I myself have experienced them. Rather than it being some kind of magic manifestation, however, to me this is a clearing of mind and energy that allows us to see certain paths or opportunities that a closed or stressed mind may have missed.

This is how I think Reiki can help us get out of a difficult situation, through clearing and alignment. But money for money's sake is a very modern concept that doesn't, by itself, value the depth, complexity and personal inner growth that comes with Reiki.

"Reiki makes you look younger"

This is another myth, and again I believe it's a misunderstanding. Certainly, this isn't what Reiki is for, and isn't the reason for Usui teaching the system! Perhaps a few people feel this to be true and have passed the idea on to their students, but as with everything Reiki, we can't guarantee that this will happen for everyone, or indeed at which stage of our lives or Reiki training we will see this apparent effect.

I believe what some people are referring to when they think of this isn't an actual defying of age, but rather the effect that Reiki has on our inner being. After working with Reiki on myself and being with clients for several hours or a full day, I have had friends say to me, "You're looking really well ... You look bright," and similar such sentiments. I believe this is the effect of working with energy, clearing us out and making us feel so good that we literally glow. Our eyes look brighter and our smiles wider – and don't we all look more beautiful when we are smiling? We have an energy about us that quietly states "positivity"! It's all of this, feeling so good on the inside that it shows on the outside, in our faces and in our body language, that "makes us look younger".

It could also be the effect that the healing has on us: clearing, cleansing and realigning, so that we actually look healthy and, some may think, younger. Indeed, in my own class when I undertook Reiki training, I vividly remember a lady in the class who was very quiet and unassuming. Our master did the *Reiju*, and afterwards when this lady stood up, the whole class gasped. Someone said what we were all thinking, "You look ten years younger!" The lady smiled and replied, "I feel it." It was remarkable, as she truly looked as if a great burden had been lifted from her, making her appear lighter, physically and energetically. This sudden, immediate physical effect of Reiki isn't something that I have ever seen occur in my own classes with students – although I have had people in joyful tears – but it's certainly a consequence of releasing old, unwanted and stagnant energy.

If Reiki really were the secret to financial success and almost eternal youth, wouldn't everyone be doing it by now? Don't trust what someone else says just because they say it – find out what is true for you. What works for you? What do you think, and feel, with Reiki? It is this, your own practice and experiences, that matter the most.

4. Reiki – What Is It Good For?

> "All things carry Yin
> yet embrace Yang.
> They blend their life breaths
> in order to produce harmony"
>
> *- Tao Te Ching*

What is Reiki good for? The standard answer that you will hear to this question is – everything! We have already discussed how Reiki, as a holistic healing practice, can help on all levels, from physical issues through to spiritual growth and development. Therefore, Reiki is good for helping and healing anything! This is all well and good, but what does this actually *mean*? Let us take a closer look.

There are two ways that we can look at Reiki and how we engage with its healing effects. We have the surface-level healing – that is, treating symptoms of a physical illness or condition – and then we have the deeper healing that occurs from the inside out, on the mental and emotional levels.

With physical healing, we can perform a Reiki hands-on healing to simply help anything from bumps and bruises or an ache or pain, to an acute condition such as a cold or a headache, through to a chronic one such as arthritis or chronic fatigue syndrome (CFS). Hands down, focus on

Reiki, and allow that energy to flow where it is needed. We begin to feel better, and that is it – it's that simple.

How does this work? Why does it work? We can't explain or answer this from a scientific point of view. Reiki itself can't be measured. People have tried, and for a while Reiki was thought to be part of the electromagnetic spectrum, but so far this hasn't been validated. We do know from anecdotal evidence that it works, helping to alleviate pain. We are connecting with universal *ki* to allow the body to heal itself, and the practitioner doesn't need to do anything else except to focus on Reiki. The receiver will experience and take from the flow of energy, this connection with Reiki, whatever it is that they need.

Reiki has been known to actually increase the amount of pain felt in a physical level of healing. The reason for this is that as the body heals, the pain is raised to the surface as it's being released. This can feel uncomfortable, and the person receiving may wish to stop. In this case, little and often sessions (if informal, i.e. not in a professional setting) would be best so to avoid causing too much discomfort. But this increase in pain for physical healing is perfectly normal and is something that I have experienced, both when giving Reiki and receiving it myself. Giving Reiki in this way aids relief from pain and eases any hurt, helping us to feel better whether our issue is a minor one-off or an ongoing condition. We could consider physical healing as surface-level healing, as it's so simple that it just flows and helps, without any deeper awareness being required.

Now let us consider Reiki from the inside out – what it can do for us beyond healing physical issues. Acceptance in Western societies is growing for the medical benefits of acupuncture, acupressure, yoga and tai chi, which are all based on the same fundamental understanding that human beings have a subtle energy dimension. So Reiki makes more sense when we liken it to such practices, even though the outward mechanics aren't the same, as Reiki requires no movement of the body or other materials (such as the needles used in acupuncture). It's the creation of a clear flow of inner energy that these practices have in common.

When we focus on Reiki, we enter into a state of simply being, exactly like meditation. We take our awareness and focus inwards, which helps to calm our mind. We cease to be distracted by external matters, and our focus becomes narrowed, intent. We stop thinking in our usual way with our normal patterns, fears and worries. This break in habitual-thought response creates a sense of calm … and that calm flows from our mind, from our being to every other aspect of self … from our mind to our thoughts … then outwards to our emotions … and then further outwards to our body, releasing tension and feelings of stress. Helping one aspect of our self to come into a state of calm naturally affects all other aspects. Our mind, thoughts, emotions and body aren't separate from each other; they are intertwined. One affects another, so negative thought patterns not only affect how we think, but in turn have an effect on our emotional state.

Thinking "I'm not good enough, I'm not worthy of love" repeated often enough will make us feel low, sad and self-critical. This negative thought and emotional response could then affect our body – the thought cycles may cause stress, which in turn creates uncomfortable sensations and even pain in our body. So we can see that our thoughts affect every level of our being. When we focus inwards with Reiki, we rid ourselves of all outer distractions, including our thought patterns, and this serves to bring our whole being into "oneness" – balance, harmony and a sense of peace. The more that we give ourselves Reiki, or have Reiki, the more our usual negative thought patterns are disrupted, breaking the cycle.

By entering into a state of calm, our body stops releasing its stress hormones and instead releases its good or "happy" hormone - endorphins- which in turn reduce the amount of physical pain that we feel. Reiki helps to switch our body from the sympathetic mode to the parasympathetic mode – in other words, we go from "fight or flight" into the "relaxation" response.

In today's society, most of us are generally quite stressed. Our time schedules, work, managing deadlines, family issues and day-to-day tasks, as well as the complications of our family and love relationships, create enough stress that triggers the fight or flight response. This is exactly the same response that our hunter-gatherer ancestors had to *"Tiger! Run or fight!"* Although our society has moved on since then, our brains haven't. Our brain can't tell the difference between the stress of facing a predator and the stress of work and family pressures.

Adrenaline is high, and most people go about their day in a fight or flight response. The problem with this is that it's meant to be a short sharp response to deal with a predator – to run or to fight – and then to drop again. But the stress of today doesn't drop; it's a low-level constant, meaning our bodies are fed continual drips of the adrenaline response, and this in itself isn't good for us. It keeps us on "high alert" mode, which is tiring, and our bodies weren't meant for this low-level constant adrenaline feed. Our rest state is the relaxation response, from the parasympathetic mode of our nervous system, which allows us to feel relaxed and calm, eat properly, have a healthy libido and sleep easily. The alert response – fight or flight – shuts down digestion, libido and sleep. Stress, therefore, feeds the high alert response, which is why many people today struggle to sleep and don't eat properly.

Reiki helps to switch off the fight or flight response and trigger the relaxation response, literally flicking the switch of our nervous system. This is why we can come out of a Reiki healing session feeling good, and why many people feel rested as if they have had a deep sleep. I have had people fall asleep on the Reiki bed, which is a response to not getting enough sleep, and as soon as the body relaxes with that flow of Reiki, then zzzz! They're gone! This is good, as I can continue with Reiki and the client still receives healing, but they are also getting the rest that their body has been craving.

Reiki as a practice also goes deeper than this. When practised regularly, it can help us to continue to develop our sense of inner balance and calm, similar to meditation. This helps us to release held anger, fear, anxiety and emotions relating to past issues. Through Reiki meditation – doing self-Reiki and spending time within the connection, not rushing through it, and *paying attention* in that space and time – we begin to reveal our innermost self, the true "me", and therefore explore ourselves at a deeper level. The very act of turning in to universal *ki*, bringing our focus towards it, creates a sense of inner peace and calm. We are connecting with what is, the true nature of being. Here, in this state, is no anger, stress, guilt, or worry…just being.

So what is Reiki good for? Creating a state of calm that helps to bring our physical, mental, emotional and spiritual self into oneness, that brings a sense of well-being on all levels.

It's worth pointing out that the state of meditative focus and sense of oneness, as both healer and as a healee or recipient, can be engendered by Reiki, and is often the state that practised healers enter into, but that *it isn't necessary for Reiki to work*. A new student, for example, won't naturally fall into a meditative state. Even without that sense of oneness, the energy will still flow. New students may not have a clue what they are doing when they begin but trust the energy that they are opening themselves up to. They put their hands on another, and their minds may be going nineteen to the dozen, and Reiki still flows.

You can be thinking about what the other person may be thinking, or the next hand positions, or how you are feeling … and Reiki will still flow. It isn't necessary to *be* in a meditative state or a state of oneness, but it's what Reiki opens within us and leads us to as we develop our practice. The recipient, too, isn't expected to enter into a meditative state. They may do, but as they are the one receiving the healing, their minds are likely to be all over the place and very busy, especially if they are new to Reiki. Yet healing will and does occur, whatever they are thinking or feeling.

The real key with Reiki is intention. It always comes back to intention. As long as we want healing to occur for the other person or for ourselves, and we open up to Reiki, thinking about it as flowing energy, or a universe light beam, or as a breath of the universe, then Reiki will flow. The deeper practice and understanding comes later, as we continue with our development.

Summary

- Reiki is like meditation and can be thought of in this sense.
- By bringing focus and calm, we can help to heal ourselves and others externally on the physical level, and internally on the mental and emotional levels.
- We can't satisfactorily quantify Reiki in terms of scientific thinking, but rather understand that we are working with *ki*, with energy or essence, that is best experienced to be understood.
- Reiki can help us to reset ourselves to the relaxation response, rather than being in the fight or flight response.
- The key with Reiki is intention: to focus on Reiki and for healing to occur.

5. The Practices Within Reiki

"The mind is wavering and restless, difficult to guard and restrain: let the wise man straighten his mind as a maker of arrows makes his arrows straight."

- *The Dhammapada*

The word "Reiki" describes both the name of the energy and the system within which we work. As a framework, Reiki has a variety of tools in place to help each of us to strengthen and deepen our practice, and therefore our understanding. Each of these tools builds upon one another to engender a greater spirit and compassion towards both ourselves and others. All of this helps us to heal in our mind and spirit, as much as in body.

The tools within the system of Reiki are:

- hands on/off healing
- the Reiki precepts
- the symbols
- meditation

Reiki also includes the *Reiju*, or attunement, that is the "spiritual blessing" the master performs to connect the student with their own Reiki. The hands-on healing is perhaps the best understood mechanism within Reiki, because it's so immediate and tangible. It is also the way in which we help others. For our personal practice, however, as well as giving ourselves hands-on healing, it's the development and engagement with the above elements that helps us to gain a fuller understanding of what Reiki really means and what it provides for us, as well those we help through healing sessions.

The Reiki precepts

The secret technique of inviting happiness
The spiritual medicine for all diseases

> *Kyo dakewa*
>
> *Ikaru na*
>
> *Shinpai suna*
>
> *Kansha shite*
>
> *Gyo o hagame*
>
> *Hito ni shinsetsu ni*

Every morning and evening join your hands in prayer
Pray these words in your heart
And chant these words with your mouth
Usui Reiki therapy for improvement of body and mind

> Just for today
>
> Do not anger
>
> Do not worry
>
> Be grateful
>
> Do your duties fully
>
> Be kind to yourself and others

The precepts – known in Japanese as the *Gokai* – were written by Usui Sensei. He wrote them in Kanji, a complex written language. Due to the complexity of Kanji in transliteration, the precepts can and have been interpreted in a number of different ways. Below are some of the alternative translations of Usui Sensei's precepts.

> *For today only,*
> *Anger not*
> *Worry not*
> *Honour your elders, teachers and parents*
> *Work hard*
> *Show compassion to yourself and others*

> *Just for today,*
> *Do not anger*
> *Do not worry*
> *Be grateful*
> *Be true to your way and your being*
> *Show gratitude*

As you can see, the first parts of the precepts don't change – they are very clear: "Do not anger" and "Do not worry". This is a gentle reminder to us to recognise our feelings and sensations, but to try and let them go, to not dwell on them.

The important essence in the precepts is:

For today only

Just this – for today. We are not asking our self to *never* get angry or worried ... but to just focus on *today only*. By focusing on today, we are in neither the past nor the future. We are bringing our attention back to *Now*, which is the only moment in time that we can control.

The change in the other words of the precepts is dependent upon the way that the Kanji are translated, so we can take whichever of the translations feels right for us. In the West, "work hard" has a different cultural meaning to what it did in 1920s Japan, and I think it comes across today as quite rigid. "Work hard" doesn't just mean in a job, but for your family, loved ones and community. In other words, be of service to yourself and to others. Personally, I love the translation of *Be true to your way and your being*. To me, this says: do what is right that is within you to do so – follow your moral and spiritual compass.

Today, the precepts have been changed by many people to be more individualistic. If you have a look on the internet, you will see that they have been recreated with the addition of "I": I *will not worry* ... I *will not anger*. There are two points to make about this. Firstly, *"will not* anger/worry" is future tense – it's taking away from the *Now*, the present. The point of the precepts is that we focus on *Now*, on the present, because this is all that we can control. We can't control the past – it's gone. We can't control the future – it hasn't arrived. But we can control *who we are and how we feel* in this very moment. "I will not anger" is a command for the future, rather than a reminder of the present. If we tell ourselves "I *will not* ..." then what about *Now*? What if we are angry *Now*? Our brains process what we say literally, so if we are angry in the present moment, telling ourselves "will not" may not take away how we are feeling *Now*.

"Do not anger ... Do not worry ..." feels like a grandfather or an aunty gently patting us on the shoulder and giving us some friendly advice! Whereas "I will not anger ..." feels more like a rigid command to the self. The difference may be subtle, but it can potentially make a profound difference in how we internalise the instructions.

Secondly is the use of *I*. From the Buddhist perspective, *I* is an illusion; it doesn't really exist; it is just a construct of our ego mind. The whole point of the Buddhist practices is to release the self of the idea of *I*, of a self separate from the whole. Therefore, I believe that Usui Sensei was very deliberate in the phrasing of the precepts, and intentionally didn't include *I*, because this brings the focus back to the self – but saying "do not anger" or "do not worry" seems to be a much gentler way of talking to the self. I think that if we change the precepts and add *I*, we are changing a nuance of their intention.

Usui Sensei instructs us to:

"pray these words in your heart and chant these words with your mouth"

and to do so morning and evening. Therefore, they were an important part of the system of Reiki, to help us to go within and to remind us of how to be kind to ourselves and to others.

It only takes five minutes to chant the precepts, or 10, or 20 ... however long you want to spend contemplating them. If you don't already work with the precepts, try doing so every day for a week and see if, at the end of that week, you notice any difference in yourself, mentally and emotionally.

Reiki symbols

A specific set of symbols are taught within Reiki classes, usually from level two (Usui Reiki). Sometimes the first symbol is included in level one training, as it is in Jikiden Reiki. Other branches of Reiki have additional levels and symbols. The original symbols were given to us by Mikao Usui, and each of them has a specific meaning. They are used as both visualisations and as mantras: that is, the names of the symbols can be chanted. Both visualisation and chanting are ways to help further enhance our understanding of Reiki. They are a form of meditation, to focus within. The symbols are also used in hands-on healings to enhance the session. Further discussion on this topic can be found in chapter 19.

Meditations

Meditation is absolutely complementary to Reiki, as these are both practices to help heal and balance our mind to achieve well-being. Meditation helps us to focus and keep our minds in control, rather than wandering here, there and everywhere. It can allow us to release distractions, as well as negative thoughts and stress. The main meditation that is taught in Reiki classes, handed down from Mikao Usui is the *Hatsurei Ho*, which is given in chapter 8. Below are some other meditations that I like to do, and that you may find beneficial.

Reiki hands-off meditation

- Sit as you usually would for meditation – in a kneeling position or in a chair with your feet flat on the floor (not crossed at the ankles or knees).
- Begin with *Gassho* (hands in prayer position).
- Stay in *Gassho*, or move your hands onto your lap, palms up.
- Breathe gently and deeply, down to your *hara* (below your navel), for a few minutes.
- Connect with Reiki. Just allow yourself to tune in, to feel Reiki.
- If you like, visualise / sense / feel breathing in Reiki, breathing out Reiki.
- As you feel that connection with Reiki, visualise / feel / sense the energy coming through your hands, and moving through you up to your head, then coming out and down in a gentle shower all around you.
- Allow that Reiki to flow, just covering you, repeating Reiki coming in through your hands – up to your head – out and down all around you – washing your whole body in Reiki.
- Repeat continually, gently aware of any sensations that you feel, physically, energetically, mentally and emotionally.
- To finish, breathe to *hara*, focus on your *hara*, just breathing here.
- Hands in *Gassho*, nice deep breath – and gently return.

You can adapt the above meditation, so that instead of Reiki flowing through your hands and up, if you are comfortable, you can simply sit "in Reiki", just feeling it, connecting with it, continuing to breathe in Reiki and breathe out Reiki. Feel it flow and move throughout your whole body. See what you notice afterwards, and how you feel.

The Heart meditation

- Sit in meditation with your hands in *Gassho*.
- Breathe deeply to *hara*.
- Place your hands on the heart centre.
- Focus on this area, just breathing gently.
- Keep your focus on the feel of your hands at your heart … allowing Reiki to flow.
- Feel / sense / visualise your heart centre opening like a flower…
- Feel as if it's expanding, then contracting just a little, expanding again and contracting…
- Visualise the light from your heart centre as white, pink or green, glowing brightly.
- Allow that Reiki to go as deep as it can at your heart, filling you up from the inside, spilling out and around your whole self.
- Let yourself experience any emotions or feelings that come through. Experience, without attachment: be as an observer, staying heart-centred in Reiki.
- Gently bring your focus back to your heart centre and the feel of your hands.
- Lower your hands and take some gentle breaths.
- Gently bring yourself back.

Grounding meditation

If you are feeling a bit "high" from all the energy work you have been doing, or a little woozy, or just need to come back into your body and feel more aware and present, this is a really good meditation.

A simple way of grounding – coming back to the whole self in the here and now – is to simply continue to breathe to your *hara*, taking your attention, focus and energy to this area. This can be a quick, useful way of bringing yourself back. There are also some longer meditations that can help as well:

- Sit in meditation (kneeling, half lotus or in a chair).
- Start by just focusing on your breath, feeling your breath moving in and out of your body.
- Hands in *Gassho* and breathe to *hara*.
- Keep your hands in *Gassho* or place them in your lap, palms up.
- Keep your attention, energy and focus on your *hara*.
- Allow that energy and focus to move downward … down from *hara* to root (located at the base of your spine).
- Allow that energy to move down from root, through your legs, to your feet.
- Feel the energy continually moving down, from *hara* to feet, every time you breathe.

You can take this further by feeling or sensing the energy moving further down…

- Going past your feet down to the ground…
- See / feel / sense the energy turning into tree roots, becoming stronger, going deeper.
- Feel those tree roots connected to the earth and connected to you, part of your energy.
- Keep your focus on this for as long as you wish to.
- Gently bring your energy back up into your feet…
- Up from your feet all the way back to your *hara*.
- Breathe gently … and bring yourself back.

By using all of the methods and tools within the system of Reiki, the hands-on/off healing, the precepts, the symbols and the meditations, we come to a far richer meaning and deeper knowledge of Reiki, and of our own whole self. The practices were designed as different methods to reach the same goal: focus, inward attention, letting go. They all reach that goal in different ways — but just as with hands-on healing, we will each experience the practices and the outcomes in our own way. We become enriched and knowledgeable, and stronger in our compassion and our being.

Summary

- Reiki is a framework within which we practise healing and self-development.
- There are a variety of tools within the system, helping us to increase our understanding and our well-being.
- These tools are the hands-on/off healing, the precepts, meditations, symbols and the *Reiju*.
- It is helpful to include all of these tools (except the *Reiju*) within our own regular Reiki practice.

6. Defining Reiki

"Well when you are hurting you put your hands on where it hurts and you say 'Reiki on' and then you keep your hands there and then you feel better."

- Devyn, aged 8

The question of being able to explain Reiki, to define it both to the satisfaction of oneself and to others, is the eternal question for Reiki students.

"But how do I explain this to my family and friends?" is a question that gets asked in every course I run. The common metaphor that is used is:

"Think of Reiki like electricity ... you can't see it, experience it in any way, until – flick – we switch the switch, and then we have light, or noise, or heat. It is the same with Reiki: it is always there, this subtle energy force, we just need to flick the switch to allow us to experience it."

This is useful to describe Reiki, but it doesn't *define* Reiki. It is difficult to give an accurate definition because of its internal and subtle nature. It makes the most sense to me personally to describe it as a "moving meditation" and that its benefits are similar to those that we gain through the practice of meditation. We have already described it as "energy healing" and "universal life force energy", as this is the closest analogy. We are working with something non-physical, non-medical, that has been seen by many to have a positive and beneficial effect holistically.

Certainly, what Reiki is *not* is massage. It isn't any kind of physical manipulation of the body. The fact that we are able to connect with others and facilitate their own healing, helping them come into that same place of oneness, of feeling better in mind, body and spirit, of aligning and rebalancing their whole self into a calm, relaxed, more healthy state is amazing, and still, essentially, indefinable.

This idea of Reiki as meditation is one way to describe it, but it isn't the whole of Reiki. We best understand it through the experience of it, through having a session of Reiki and continuing our own development. There comes a point when we realise that naming and labels only get us so far, and that it is okay to drop them. Each person will discover their own way of being able to define Reiki in a way that fits with them.

For Reiki to make sense to my conscious, analytical brain, I have boiled it down to three essentials:

Intention

Connection

Compassion

The *intention* to connect with Reiki; with universal energy … the *intention* to go within, to focus on the inner self. Once we set our intention, we *connect* with Reiki; with *ki* – both within ourselves and the great *ki* of the universe. Once we have connected, then it is our *compassion* – and our *intention* – that allows us to heal ourselves and others. How can healing take place without compassion? How can we help others to heal if we don't like them, or don't want to do the session? Compassion and intention are key! The same goes for our own self too – to have compassion for our own self-healing to take place.

We may not start off with compassion. Indeed, we may not even be aware of it. Yet, the more that we practise Reiki, the more that we are led into that sense of compassion, the stronger our compassion becomes. Reiki *is* compassion.

Think about it: how do you feel when you are sitting in Reiki meditation? How do you feel when you are receiving Reiki or self-healing or healing others? Do we feel despair, pain, anger, hate? No. Do we feel bubbly, happy, excited? Not usually. The sense of holistic balance that we feel isn't a strong emotion: strong emotions can't last, they fizz and die out, because they are surface emotions and can't be sustained. What is left underneath those surface emotions is quiet contentment; peace; *compassion*. We begin to understand the concept of no-separation, and of all energy as one. Reiki leads us to understanding – and strengthening – true compassion. These three words are the spirit of the definition of Reiki.

Reiki is healing

This is how Reiki is usually defined – that it's a healing modality. Let us take a close look at this word *healing*. What is actually meant by this? We all assume that we mean the same thing, but the word has connotations and therefore it is subjective rather than objective. So, within Reiki, what does *healing* actually mean?

Healing – a way to make better. To feel better. To make aches and pains go away; to recover from illness or sickness; to no longer feel sad, angry, guilty, scared, anxious.

However, it can also mean something else: instead of *making better*, it can also mean to make whole, to bring into wholeness. This isn't the same as necessarily making the bad stuff, physically or mentally, disappear, but rather that we come to a place of *acceptance and balance*. That we begin to accept what is, rather than wishing it were not. We accept who and what we are, or our current circumstances. We begin to have a new vision, a new clarity of mind that helps us to accept the situation in which we find ourselves. In so doing, healing isn't about recovery per se, but about having a healthier mind state.

Reiki can of course help "to make better". Many sessions end with people finding that physical symptoms are minimised or have disappeared altogether, that mental stress and anxiety is lessened. But has it gone completely? Can we "fix" underlying chronic health conditions? No, this isn't the case, so in this sense Reiki healing doesn't "make better"…but it does help to bring peace to our being, and a sense of acceptance and balance – in other words, healing into wholeness.

Reiki healing is also spiritual growth: it helps us to grow into ourselves, to develop internally, as a whole person. This is also a true definition. Reiki is spiritual healing – or at least it can be, if we choose to develop our path in that way. Spiritual growth isn't necessarily about taking away whichever ills we suffer, but to be the person that we are with them, and to be able to see and to define ourselves beyond them. Healing is growing in some way, growing from illness, or sadness or despair; growing *around* our chronic illness or trauma; growing *deeper* with our own self, knowing ourselves more, becoming more comfortable with ourselves, and it could be said that all of this is spiritual healing, or spiritual growth.

Reiki healing is all of these things and is defined by the experience that each of us has on our journey. But if our expectation of it is simply "to cure our ills", I think we risk narrowing the true depth and complexity of Reiki, and of the richness with which it can enhance our whole self.

The other point that we need to take into consideration is the difference of experience between a student of Reiki and a person receiving a healing session. A student of Reiki should ideally be practising all of the elements within the system of Reiki – self healing; the precepts; meditation; and at higher levels, the symbols and mantras. All of these together create an experience that develops the self, internally and externally, in mind and body. We begin to see the expansion of compassion, spiritual growth and positive changes in our mental state.

A person who comes for a healing session (who isn't trained in Reiki) gets one hour or so of Reiki healing, without the background of the training or the practice. Therefore, their experience is based solely on the sensations during the treatment, the discussion with the practitioner, and how they feel afterwards. We could say that, in a sense, their experience of Reiki is much simpler: it's evident only from the hands-on (or off) physical treatment. This is why we tend to call Reiki "healing" in the sense of "making better", because this is how the recipient would perceive it, unless they have other experiences alongside the treatment.

One session for a client isn't going to expand their sense of spiritual self or help them to feel that they are going deeper into themselves as a person. If, however, that person chooses to continue having regular Reiki sessions, deeper layers of healing may begin to emerge, particularly the perception of the mental and emotional state and beginning to recover from long-held wounds or difficult circumstances. The more a person becomes familiar with Reiki, the more that the "wholeness" and "spiritual growth" aspects unfold for them.

How a recipient of Reiki perceives the healing effect is, of course, dependent upon their own circumstances. Someone who meditates regularly, and perhaps does tai chi or yoga or similar, will already be aware of energy and of themselves as more than the physical self. Therefore, they are more likely to understand the deeper layers of Reiki healing and be more aware of what it is they are experiencing. The same is true of someone who comes to Reiki without this knowledge, but is completely open and aware of their own sense of spirituality. But someone who "just wants to get better" may perceive the experience as just that – feeling better.

For something that is so simple on the surface, Reiki can bring a variety of experiences, as it helps on an individual basis for that person and their personal needs at that time, and each of us will take from it what we are open to understanding.

Reiki creates the conditions for healing to occur...

There is a saying – that Reiki helps to create the conditions for healing to occur, that it's actually the person's own body that does the healing. This is the official description generally given to describe Reiki, and this is certainly true ... but it isn't the whole truth. When we give Reiki to ourselves or another, the mind and body come into balance, and healing that is needed at that time occurs from within, allowing the body to create its own healing. However, there are times when we may get a feeling of intensity at certain points, as though we are soaking Reiki up like a sponge, going right through our body into a deeper part of ourselves. A deep healing is occurring; one that feels like something other than just our own body healing itself. How do we define this? Is it spiritual? It can certainly feel like that, on occasion, but not in every case. Or is it our mind, or our energy? All of it, perhaps?

I feel that this essence of intense energy, where heat and sensations are strong and deep and being sucked in by something within our essence, is indefinable through the medium of language. We can attempt a definition, but that definition becomes a *truth*, not *the* truth. It is the experience that we take from it that matters, not the labelling of the thing.

"... Naming is a necessity for order
but naming can not order all things.
Naming often makes things impersonal,
so we should know when naming should end.
Knowing when to stop naming,

Defining Reiki

you can avoid the pitfall it brings."
Tao Te Ching (Laozi and McDonald, 2010)

Sometimes the healing can feel so deep and profound that we can't define it. It's enough to experience it and know that we are healing. This is what I hope is passed on to others:

- that Reiki is simple yet complex
- that it's healing through balance and wholeness
- that it helps and affects every level of us
- that it can be a different experience for everyone
- that it's the experience of what we feel both during the treatment and in the days and even weeks afterwards that matter
- that it can be a "making better", but not always
- that "healing" is more than a simple "making better", that can be different for each person

To explain Reiki in a way that we ourselves can understand, and that others may also understand, healers use phrases such as: "I turn Reiki on and off as I need it," or "I channel Reiki to come through me." These phrases can help our rational mind get to grips with understanding energy, but they are not wholly accurate. We don't need to "turn Reiki on" because it's always there. I think of it as the spiritual equivalent of air: just *being*, just *there*. We don't "call it in". We simply need to connect with what is already around us, and we do this by tuning in to it, by turning our attention to it. It's a bit like realising that we are breathing: we don't spend our whole day consciously breathing, it simply happens as we go about our day, working and shopping and meeting people. Then occasionally we may become conscious of our breathing: we may sit for a few minutes and enjoy the feel of breathing in and out.

This is also why we need to bring our focus and attention to Reiki, because we are so distracted by our daily activities that we don't realise innate Reiki is already there within each of us. By stopping and deliberately turning our attention towards it, we become aware, and so we can immediately access it. We simply step into the connection of Reiki, bringing our intention to that connection, as it's the intention that really is the driving force in the healing process. I use this term "step into the connection" throughout this book, as an alternative to "channelling" or "turning Reiki on" because this is a more accurate description for what we do. We become aware of Reiki, which is just there – being.

Summary

- We can describe Reiki as a moving meditation, as it has similar effects and benefits, although Reiki itself is more than meditation.
- We can think of Reiki as: intention; connection; compassion.
- The term "healing" can mean several things: to make better; to heal into wholeness; spiritual growth.
- Reiki creates the conditions for our body to heal itself…
- …Yet the healing can feel deeper than this, in a way that is difficult to define, so we each take our own personal experience from Reiki.

7. Questions, Questions!

**"Forging a true way,
expectations at last gone.
In this the soul shines."**

- Julian Bound, 'Haiku'

I see so many questions about Reiki on social media forums. For example:

- "My teacher never told me about…"
- "I can't feel anything, does this mean it isn't working?"
- "Is it true that….?"
- "How do I know I am doing it right?"

The same questions seem to circulate over and over again. Does this mean that a Reiki teacher isn't doing a good job? Does this mean that the student hasn't been paying attention? The answer in both cases is – no! Or at least, not necessarily! As Reiki has travelled through time and cultures, it has taken on new adaptations, meanings and additions, and therefore there can be a lot to learn and take on board.

The usual format of Reiki training is that each level is taught over a one- or two-day period. Personally, I teach each level over two days. This is enough time to explain the mechanics of Reiki, the theory underlying it, the hows and whys, and the practical application of meditations and healing. Reiki is an easy methodology to learn as the technique is simple. However, understanding it as a meditative and holistic treatment, and even as a spiritual practice, is much deeper, and it can take years to comprehend.

Think about meditation: it's simple to learn *how* to meditate – sit down, close your eyes, remain quiet, breathe and focus inwards. But what meditation actually teaches us, what it does for us, and the long-term benefits that it can bring can't be learnt in one day, nor one week, nor even one month! We continue to practise meditation on a regular basis for years (and years!) because it *continues to be of benefit every single time* – and just like with Reiki, the effect of the practice is accumulative: that is, we reap more positive benefits from doing it as we continue to practise regularly, and our understanding grows with the practice. Meditation and Reiki – and also other beneficial practices such as yoga and tai chi – help to de-stress our mind and body and shape them with positive thoughts. Over time we find that we are more easily able to deal with challenging situations, because we have a healthy and balanced mental state.

Each time we practise Reiki, for ourselves as well as for others, we learn more, we learn again, and we continue to learn, about both the nature of Reiki and our deeper self, at our inner core.

This then being true, how can we expect to learn everything there is to learn in a two-day workshop? We can't. Reiki training isn't like a class in maths or English! There is no knowing everything; there are no absolutes! Would you expect to learn everything about karate or tai chi in a day or a week? Reiki training isn't about learning everything: it's about learning *enough* to then continue your own journey and development. It's better to think of Reiki classes as a jumping off point, or a foundation for learning. It's the beginning point from which a student then continues their own practice. And yes, questions will always arise … because, as human beings, our emotions change again and again. Our thinking and our feelings are constantly changing ... we are different from one day to the next, let alone one year to the next! The challenges and situations that we encounter are constant. Every time we sit down and do Reiki, it will feel different, or we will have different thoughts about what it is that we are experiencing. It's only natural that at every level, from beginners to experienced masters, questions will always arise.

There is also another factor – the additional tools and systems that now get added alongside Reiki.

Reiki as a system, created in 1920s Japan, was in a different time and culture to the Western world today. In every Japanese discipline, your teacher told you to do something, and you did it, no question. Action came first; explanation after. It was cultural not to question your teacher. What was taught was direct, and in a sense, pure. This teaching was handed down from master to student, who became master, and therefore taught in exactly the same way.

Not only do we have a different way of teaching today – very much asking questions of what we are taught, for one! – but we have a plethora of beliefs, and our understanding of "energy" and all associated matters is of course quite different to how the Japanese would have understood them in Usui's time. Therefore, teachers and students of all branches of Reiki may now add things that wouldn't have been part of Usui's original teachings. For example: angels, crystals, spirit entities, psychic abilities and psychic attachments. These come up quite often in relation to Reiki today but wouldn't have been a part of the original training under Usui in Japan.

Some teachers will focus on "Angel Reiki" or "Crystal Reiki", while others may not, according to their own personal experiences and beliefs. Some teachers may talk about the psychic elements of Reiki – others won't. Some focus purely on the very physical and mechanical aspects of Reiki, while others may focus on mental and emotional well-being, and still others will talk more about the spiritual element.

A Question of Reiki

So you see, Reiki isn't as simple as we first thought! I am not saying that there is a wrong or a right when it comes to practising and teaching Reiki, just that today's teachings are much more varied in scope from its original source, which creates different focus points and understanding. You can see from this, then, that as a student develops their own Reiki journey, they are naturally going to come across information they weren't taught in their training. It's up to each one of us to decide what we feel we want to take on board, and what doesn't fit with our own beliefs.

The recent popularity in Reiki is of course an incredibly good thing. If everyone in the world practised Reiki, I think we would have more emotionally balanced, compassionate and self-aware adults – and children too! I think it's wonderful that Reiki and other holistic complementary practices are becoming more accepted. However, so much information now floats about that people can become confused with what *is* Reiki and what *isn't* Reiki. For example, as stated earlier in chapter 3, the idea that "Reiki makes you look younger!" or "Can I have Reiki to help my finances?" If these were one of the first pieces of information you came across when researching Reiki, you would have quite a different view of it!

The same is true for questions asked on social media about "psychic attacks", "spirit entities", "seeing someone's past", and so on. These *may* come into someone's development alongside their Reiki practice, but these are *not part of Reiki*, as is. Suffice it to say that some people have been scared of undertaking Reiki training because they have been told, or they have seen on the internet, that Reiki can make you aware of psychic attacks or that you start to work with spirit entities. This isn't true.

Reiki has nothing to do with esoteric work unless someone is already interested in developing this. Reiki is simply healing – it needs only our intention, our focus, and to tune in to the underlying energy. I will discuss these additional elements in later chapters. For now, let us concentrate on the general questions about Reiki. Most of these questions have a few simple answers…

Time

Patience

Practice
Practice
Practice

It really is this simple. I have been working with Reiki for over sixteen years, and I am still learning. My understanding of Reiki, as a system and a practice, has gone through several alterations because I keep learning, and we can only learn about Reiki by *doing*. By doing the practices. Reading helps too! But *there are no shortcuts!*

Don't be in such a hurry! Why do you want to know everything there is to know about Reiki immediately? Slow down – enjoy the journey! Practise, learn, discover! We understand so much more when we discover it through our own learning. Someone else can tell you that $x=y$, and that A happens because of B, but we don't often understand this until we see it for ourselves. We may have the intellectual understanding, but not the heart of the understanding.

Not sure what you should be feeling? Keep practising (there is no right or "should", by the way: there is simply what is).

Not sure if what you are feeling is right? Keep practising (again, there is no right or "should").

Not sure if Reiki is working for you? Keep practising (does meditation always work the first, second, third time you do it?)

"Practice, practice, practice" is the answer to most questions! Be patient; allow yourself to experience whatever it is that is happening. Understanding will follow. Slow that mind down … Just be!

Summary

- The practice of Reiki can throw up a lot of questions. This is due to the varied nature of modern beliefs and culture.
- Teachers will focus on different aspects of Reiki training and information according to their own experiences and beliefs.
- There can be a lot of misunderstanding and misinformation out on social media about Reiki.

- Reiki involves ongoing patient development, and it's up to each individual to find what is right for them.
- Time, patience, and practice, practice, practice!

8. It's All In The Hands

"Where is the self when no one is thinking about it?"

- Chris Niebauer, Ph.D. 'No Self, No Problem'

"Reiki comes from the hands."

This is a phrase that gets repeated a lot. It refers to the sensations that we feel in our hands as we give Reiki, such as heat, tingling or pulsing. These sensations can help us to verify that energy is flowing as they are a tangible and physical effect. However, when we truly understand Reiki, we begin to see that this idea, this phrase, is inaccurate.

We perform Reiki by laying our hands on or just off the body. It's because of this act that people say Reiki comes from our hands, but what is really happening is that we *feel* Reiki through our hands, as these are the focus point. When we consider that Reiki is universal or spiritual energy, we understand that energy is already there, all around us. This *ki* is both without and within; it's everywhere. We focus, we breathe, we let go of all distractions. We set our minds to the connection, to being with Reiki, and we let it flow. Therefore, Reiki comes *through* the hands, but not *from* the hands: we are simply using our hands to focus intention.

Reiki comes from – and through – our whole being. A great way to practise understanding this is through the meditation *Hatsurei Ho*. This practice, handed down from Usui Sensei, is given at the end of this chapter.

I don't feel anything in my hands – does that mean it isn't working?

This is a common question. As our hands are the focal point of giving Reiki, they may begin to warm up during a session, starting from a very gentle "just above body temperature" heat, increasing to very hot and almost painful. It can be great to feel this heat, or tingling or pulsing, as it's a measure of the Reiki energy. In today's society, it's almost as though we *need* this confirmation for proof that something is really happening. However, we should be cautious with this, and there are several factors to consider that may affect this sensation in our hands. Just because you don't feel anything doesn't mean that nothing is happening. It doesn't mean that you have failed, or that you are not doing – or can't do – Reiki.

The factors to consider when we think about sensations through our hands are:

- conscious/unconscious barriers
- more sensations – more healing
- what happens after – the real effect of Reiki
- everyone is different

Let us look at each of these factors in turn.

Conscious/Unconscious barriers:

Reiki is different from anything else in our culture. It can't be measured or quantified. We can't see it or smell it. In a way we simply have to accept it, trusting what we feel physically and through any effect we may perceive mentally or emotionally. It can take some time for our brain, which is used to rationalising and analysing, to let go and just accept. Even if we, as a new student, come to Reiki with belief and willingness, the brain may have different ideas! It takes time to unravel the barriers – whether conscious or unconscious – that have built up over our life experience. Continuing to practise helps with this. Just accept that what happens, happens – without judgement, or attachment.

I have had students who, on the training course, don't feel anything when they do self-Reiki. Yet when they give healing to another student, they suddenly feel sensations in their hands. It is a wonderful feeling for them, like a light bulb moment. Sometimes it's harder to accept Reiki for ourselves. We don't let go to begin with, in the same way that we can focus on healing another. Perhaps we feel at some level that we don't deserve the benefits of Reiki – perhaps we don't feel worthy of healing, of acceptance, of inner peace; perhaps we can't accept this for ourselves. Or another consideration may be that perhaps we have too high an expectation of what we should be feeling – something obvious and overt, like lightning bolts coming from our hands! – and when we don't feel that, then we think nothing is happening. The flow of energy can feel very subtle, and we are not always tuned in enough to recognise it. The gentle signals may be missed due to our own assumptions and expectations. Giving Reiki to another is a useful way of being able to understand that the energy is there, and that we can indeed tune in to universal *ki*.

It's also the case that some students don't feel anything when they give Reiki to another, yet the person receiving the healing does feel sensations during the treatment, such as tingling in areas of their body, or waves of energy, or they may feel that the practitioner's hands are really, really hot (even if the practitioner doesn't feel their own hands are hot). Their feedback to the practitioner is valuable in confirming that Reiki is being received.

Just because you as the healer don't feel any sensations through your hands doesn't mean that nothing is happening. The person receiving Reiki may be feeling strong sensations, even if you are not aware of it. This is why we typically leave our hands in place for at least five minutes on each position on the body – to allow Reiki to do what it does, and for the receiver to experience what is needed.

The giving of Reiki to another is not about us as the healer, it isn't about ego. It's about allowing what needs to happen for that person, whatever that experience may be. The healer and the healee may both feel exactly the same sensations in the same area; for example, strong heat at the heart centre (chakra or energy centre), pulsing at the solar plexus, and so on. Or it may be that each feels something different at the positions – the healer may feel strong heat coming from their hands at the sacral centre, yet the recipient may feel it as a cold sensation, or as a tingling. The sensations experienced don't matter so much as the strength and the location of it. This indicates that Reiki is flowing at this point, and that balancing of whatever it is that the client needs is occurring. It's interesting to discuss together and to compare, but there is no need to try and label or pin attachments to the experience.

Some students don't feel anything at all until they have been home, in their own comfortable environment, and then after a few days of practising hands-on healing for themselves or family or friends, they suddenly become aware of the sensations. It can take time, practice and patience! The more that we simply accept, without judgement or expectation, the easier it is to drop the conscious or unconscious barriers.

More sensations – more healing

We won't always feel sensations in our hands when practising Reiki, and this is because the sensations are linked with the amount of healing that the body part or chakra (energy centre) we are focused on actually needs. The more healing or balance that is needed at a particular point, the stronger the sensation is likely to be.

If we have our hands on a certain area that is well balanced, with nothing at all wrong, then we won't feel any heat, tingling or pulsing at that area. It's best to leave the hands in position for at least several minutes, to ensure that this is the case. Sometimes it can take a little while for the energy to be felt, for things to begin to flow, especially when we are new to Reiki, or if we are not quite centred in ourselves at the beginning of the session.

If we still feel nothing after five minutes or so, we can move to the next area. This may heat up intensely, giving a different feel from the previous position. This heat can indicate that a lot of re-balancing is needed at this area – and that healing may be physical, mental or emotional. Each area, or point, or chakra, may give us a different intensity of heat or sensations.

If we don't feel much at all throughout the whole session, we may presume that the person, including ourselves if it's self-Reiki, is pretty well balanced and actually didn't need much Reiki. An alternative consideration may be that the healing or energy has had a subtle effect, and that the changes may be experienced softly, slowly and gently, rather than immediately and profoundly. We can only know this in how things manifest or change over the next few days and weeks.

Conversely, if we find that our hands feel very hot throughout the whole session, at every area, and with pulsing or tingling also happening, then we can take it as a sign that a lot of healing and re-balancing is taking place. Perhaps the person has an illness or underlying condition; perhaps they have been experiencing a lot of stress or emotional turmoil. The reasons are as varied as the individuals.

Intense sensations throughout the whole session will indicate that the person is receiving healing holistically, on all levels. It has been my experience that physical pains or issues produce a lot of heat during a healing, so someone with a sprained ankle or a shoulder problem will feel a lot of heat at that area. As the healer, it's best to keep our hands in that position, on the painful area, until the sensation of heat in our hands has calmed down.

Depending on the circumstances, though, this may not be possible – a serious issue is going to take a lot longer to clear, and a professional practitioner can end up spending the whole session on this one area, as the heat doesn't calm down because the receiver's body is continuing to take as much energy as is needed in this instance. We can have a discussion with our client as to what is best for them – do you want me to focus just on this area today, or to have a balanced Reiki session, going from head to foot – or to specific areas? We can be guided by both our client and our own intuition, about what is best in that particular circumstance.

Tadao Yamaguchi, in his book *Light on the Origins of Reiki*, describes the levels of sensations as a specific order depending upon the amount of healing required. It starts from a gentle heat, indicating a little healing. If the heat increases in intensity and the hands feel quite hot, this tells us that more healing is taking place. This may increase again to a tingling feeling in the hands or on the client's body, as even more Reiki is needed, and this sensation may cycle two or three times, fading and then restarting again. If the practitioner's hands begin to feel like they are throbbing or pulsing, this is deeper healing, and a lot of Reiki is required. The final stage of sensations is that of the practitioner feeling pain in their hands, and even travelling up the arms. This may be indicative of a serious issue or pain being experienced by the client, and a lot of attention is needed at this area.

Occasionally a cold sensation may be felt instead of heat. Yamaguchi says that this falls between the throbbing and the pain sensations, and it should change from cold to warm as Reiki is given. He describes that according to Jikiden Reiki they expect any sensation to cycle several times per position, so hands are kept in position even after the strength of the sensation fades, as more Reiki may be required. This isn't something often described or taught in Western Usui Reiki: once a sensation fades, we tend to move to the next area.

How long we keep our hands in each position really depends upon:

- intuition
- how you were taught and what branch of Reiki you follow
- how much time you have to complete the session

A healing session for someone really does depend on these factors, often including the use of intuition for what feels right at that time. Reiki isn't prescriptive, but many teachers and practitioners will have their own way of performing a treatment. What is right for you will come with time, and it will likely change as you develop your practice. To enhance your confidence, and to understand this further, I reiterate what I said earlier – read a variety of books on Reiki. Think about your own training and the way that you were taught, and perhaps, if possible, attend a local Reiki share, which can be valuable in sharing knowledge and techniques. And of course ...*practice, practice, practice!*

What happens after – the real effect of Reiki

People can get very caught up in the Reiki treatment itself, wanting to experience sensations, or even psychic phenomenon. This is entirely natural, but it isn't the point of giving Reiki, either to ourselves or another person. It's difficult not to feel disappointed if you haven't felt any sensations during the Reiki treatment. It's even more disappointing if the recipient comes out of it and says they haven't felt anything. It's easy to begin doubting yourself, and to doubt Reiki. But here is something that I explain to my own students:

"The treatment of Reiki, for ourselves and for others is the first step. The point of doing the practice, the physical hands-on session, is not the session itself and what we may or may not feel, but what we experience and what changes may be experienced afterwards. After the treatment – how do you feel? Does your mind feel calmer, emptier, with less 'chitter-chatter' going on in there? How does your body feel? Are any aches and pains less? Symptoms calmed down? Headache gone, for example? Do you generally feel better? How do you feel emotionally? Do you feel calmer? Less stressed than before? Less angry, less guilty...? Do you feel more balanced, more grounded?"

This is what we need to check on – this is the point of doing the session of Reiki in the first place! To help us to feel more balanced, centred and "one" within. We can check this internal diagnostic with our self after a self-Reiki session and it should be fairly easy to determine how we feel. With others, we may need to talk them through this – to ask them these questions – because most people aren't used to checking internally and necessarily understanding their own inner state. It isn't until they are asked "how does your mind feel?" that they notice it does, indeed, feel calmer and empty of the usual bustling thoughts.

Also remember that your client or recipient may feel a little odd after a Reiki session – woozy or dozy, or not even know how they are feeling – as it's such an unusual and different sensation. They may not be able to express their feelings or understanding without a little prompting, especially if this is their first session.

Remember also that the effects of Reiki may manifest some time after the session, rather than immediately. It may take a few hours or days, or even weeks. Most people that I see as clients report feeling changes or noticing differences up to a week after the session, and often things calm down after that, though a few people may notice or experience changes in themselves or their life up to a few weeks afterwards. Everyone is different, and Reiki works with the individual's energy system, so there is no hard and fast rule with feeling the effects after a session. It's best to discuss this with the recipient, to warn them what to expect and what may occur. Otherwise, these different experiences, these emotional or physical changes, may come as a shock, particularly if they are strong or profound. Sometimes it can be subtle, unfurling gently and slowly.

Some people have a strong reaction to a Reiki treatment after their first session. Their eyes light up and they may be aware of something going on, without being able to express it verbally. Some people may take several sessions to understand their subtle energy system, and to feel the effects of Reiki. This may be because of the "unconscious barriers" in place, or maybe they are a little disassociated from their inner life, their inner being. Reiki is so different from anything else that it can be hard for someone new to it to understand what they have experienced. But another session or two should see them becoming more aware of the whole experience and start to understand any changes and re-balancing that may be occurring.

It's also worth noting that, although Reiki doesn't have any contraindications in the way that medicines do, it can bring emotions or physical manifestations of the clearing of energy to the surface. After a Reiki session, we or our clients may feel unusually tired or want to have a cry, have a headache, or experience a sudden irritability or burst of anger. Physical pain may arise, or sensations that feel weird. All of this is natural; it's simply the energy that was held inside, that is no longer needed, being raised to the surface to clear and release – like opening a floodgate to let excess water through.

Whether physical or emotional, these sensations don't last long; once released, we should find that we feel much better, lighter and clearer. However, if this isn't expected, it can come as a shock and feel overwhelming. Therefore, it's best to explain this possibility to our clients or recipients before we begin the session, so that they are aware and know what to expect. If the potential for these after-effects isn't explained, the recipient may be caught off-guard and mistake the sudden sense of anger, tiredness or "weird feelings" as the fault of Reiki, or of the practitioner, instead of understanding it as a clearing process. Old energy needs to move and release in order for healing to occur.

It may be that Reiki starts off feeling intense, but with further sessions that intensity begins to diminish and the energy and changes are more subtle. It's possible that this is due to Reiki firstly clearing the surface layers of what needs healing, and then going deeper, to older emotional wounds and long-stored issues.

The changes that are needed for an individual – the healing – is the purpose of the Reiki session: not what we as the healer feel or experience. Which brings us to another point: that what we do (as the healer) is at most only half of the story. The person receiving the session (yes, including ourselves), has responsibility for their healing too. What are they willing to accept? How much healing will they accept? Healing is a two-way street.

If your session feels disappointing, or your client says they didn't get anything from it – try not to worry or overthink it. Reiki works for our highest good, always, even if we are not aware of what that "good" means in an individual case. The client may have unconscious or conscious barriers to get through, or perhaps they have other work to do to help with their own healing journey. Maybe they are being nudged to start taking some responsibility for themselves, or to examine certain issues surrounding them. A conversation with them may reveal certain factors in their life that need examining a little more deeply. It may even be that Reiki isn't right for them at this particular time.

We must remember that Reiki isn't a miracle cure, and it won't fix or magically instantly heal a serious mental, emotional or physical condition. Some people may, despite what they say, not be ready to accept healing. There are numerous complex factors around this: some people, for example, may identify with their current state and not be sure who they are without it, so they may be frightened of accepting getting better in some way.

If a healing session feels disappointing, or doesn't go the way you expect, don't take it personally. Remember: no judgements, no attachments. Is there anything you could learn from that session? Is there anything you could have done differently? You can always ask if they are willing to try another session or two and see if anything changes. The experiences after the Reiki session, what changes are felt at any level, are far more important than the session itself. So, if you don't feel any heat or sensations in your hands, don't worry. It is the after-effects of Reiki that matter.

We don't need to get hung up on the session itself and what happens. Just like with meditation, the only bad session is the one that you don't do. The benefits may be subtle, unknown at this time, yet the accumulation of habitual practice can help to change things that aren't obvious at first, such as slowing down a frantic mind and lessening worries. Even just giving ourselves the space and time for a half hour or more of Reiki on a regular basis can be a positive experience, bringing a non-doing period into our busy lives and helping to slow things down a little, and bring us some peace.

Everyone is different

We are all different, and the sum of our experiences, expectations and assumptions will feed into how we practise and come to know Reiki. In life, some of us learn best through doing; some through listening; some through visual representation. Those who learn best through practical means, who make sense of the world through doing, feeling and experiencing, will probably feel strong sensations in their hands, because this is linked to doing. Those who are more analytical, studying and rationalising, may be less likely to experience sensations through their hands as that isn't necessarily how the world makes sense to them. This, of course, isn't a catch-all for everyone but a suggestive example. We all tune into ourselves in different ways, so experiencing Reiki will be part of that. Just because you, or someone you know, doesn't feel sensations through their hands, this doesn't mean that nothing is happening.

It's great to feel heat in our hands, as this can be a helpful indicator during a session, but don't allow yourself to get hung up on this as a sign of whether someone is a "great" Reiki healer. As we are all different, our awareness of Reiki both as a practitioner and a recipient will be experienced in a very individual way. Just realise that you can't do Reiki wrong! Whatever you experience is the experience. Just be in that moment, without worry.

Summary

- As Reiki is universal *ki*, it comes through and from our whole being.
- Our hands are the focal point of Reiki, so Reiki comes through rather than from our hands.
- Sensations felt during the session are generally indicative of the amount of healing and re-balancing required.
- What we feel during a Reiki session doesn't matter so much as what we or the recipient feel after the session, either immediately or up to a few weeks afterwards.
- Feeling sensations in the hands doesn't happen to everyone, and it isn't a sign of a successful or "great" Reiki healer.

Exercise: Hatsurei Ho

Hatsurei Ho is a meditation practice that has been handed down from Mikao Usui. It's taught in Reiki classes by many teachers. It's split into three separate parts and can be completed as a whole meditation or in its component parts.

Kenyoku Ho

- Start with *Gassho* – your hands held at your chest in prayer position. Allow your mind to calm, become clear, going within.
- Your right hand on left shoulder. Breathe in. Then on the out breath, sweep diagonally to your opposite hip.
- Your left hand to right shoulder. Breathe in. Then on the out breath, sweep diagonally to your opposite hip.
- Repeat again with your right hand to left shoulder.
- Your left arm held out in front, elbow tucked in to the side. Breathe in. Then on the out breath, with your right hand, sweep your left arm from your elbow to your fingertips.
- Repeat on the other side (your right arm held out, sweeping your elbow to your fingertips with your left hand).
- Repeat again on the first side – your left arm held out, your right hand sweeping.
- Finish with *Gassho*.

Joshin Kokyu Ho

- Hands in your lap, palms up.
- As you breathe in, feel energy coming in through your nose, and take the energy and your mind down to the *hara* (just below your navel), expanding your energy and mind through your whole body.

- As you breathe out, expand your energy and mind out of your body, continuing to expand outwards.
- Repeat until you have finished – for five to 30 minutes.
- Finish with *Gassho*.

Seishin Toitsu

- *Gassho*.
- Focus on *hara*. Breathe in, and bring energy in through your hands, through your body, to *hara*.
- Breathe out, and bring energy back up from *hara* through your body, and out through your hands.
- Repeat until you have finished – for five to 30 minutes.

The reason that we include *Hatsurei Ho* as part of our Reiki practice is that it helps us to go within, to learn to control and focus our mind, and to rid ourselves of external distractions and the constant wanderings of the mind. This helps us when in Reiki hands-on healing to maintain our focus and not become distracted by unnecessary thoughts.

It helps us to connect with our self, anchoring our body and mind together – becoming centred and whole, and therefore also grounded. It's also good practice for becoming familiar with our energy. As we focus on our *hara* and we bring the energy in and out from this point, we also focus on the feel and awareness of our energy, and how to expand it. You will notice, as you continue to develop this practice, that you can actually take your energy further outwards from your body. You will also notice that the whole process becomes far more natural and easier to do, until you simply become one with your energy, with your whole self.

9. The Reiki Trance

"The mind cannot penetrate meditation; where mind ends, meditation begins."

- Osho (Living Dangerously)

I love this strange phenomenon that I call the Reiki trance. This occurrence sometimes happens during a healing, both for ourselves and for others.

What is the Reiki trance? It's this: you start to do self-Reiki or you are having a treatment, and you are really relaxed. You think you are awake because you are aware of your environment, of noise, of thoughts in your head. But then suddenly you come to and realise that although you have been aware of your environment, you have also at the same time actually been asleep! You are suddenly startled back to full attention, usually through a change in noise level or a new noise or action.

Or it may be that you are doing self-Reiki and get to the heart position, again aware of your thoughts etc, then realise that someone is breathing deeply or snoring … and you realise that it's you! You are literally hearing yourself (gently!) snore! This awareness suddenly brings you back awake … and you have no idea how long you have been there, with your hands on your heart.

It's quite possible for this to happen a second time – you move your hands to the next position and whump! You are gone again!

The most bizarre thing about this, I think, is the fact that we don't know we have fallen asleep until something brings us back around. Our mind is telling us that we are still awake! It is one of the most curious elements I have come across in Reiki, and it still makes me giggle. In no other aspect of my life have I ever heard myself snoring. I know that we sometimes wake ourselves up during sleep when we begin to snore loudly … but with Reiki, we can gently become aware of the fact that we are snoring, continuing to snore until we are startled back to full consciousness! This happens to clients too, who mention this bizarre feeling when we finish the session.

They don't call it a "Reiki trance" because they are not sure what has happened, but they describe this curious state of being aware of their surroundings and then suddenly feeling like they have just woken up, or that they heard themselves breathing deeply or snoring. So what is it that is actually happening here? What is this "Reiki trance"?

Firstly, I believe that so many of us today don't get as much rest as we really need, both physically and mentally. We are working too much, both at jobs and as family members, either as parents or carers, or both. We go out, we meet social obligations, we are on the computer catching up with things … so when we do have the chance to fully rest during a Reiki treatment, including self-Reiki, we immediately go into a deep relaxation. It literally turns off our surface awareness. In this way, Reiki can do its thing without our ego mind getting in the way, throwing up thoughts and questions. Reiki literally acts like a switch, turning us off, so that we can get full relaxation and rest from the session.

Secondly, I think the fact that we are still aware on some level shows that we aren't fully asleep, but in a meditative-like trance state. I believe that this is what we need, at the given time, to receive the most benefit from Reiki.

> *"Because meditation is not an achievement – it is already the case, it is your nature. It has not to be achieved; it has only to be remembered. It is there waiting for you – just a turning in, and it is available. You have been carrying it always and always."*
>
> (Osho, 2015)

Sometimes during Reiki, we can fall asleep. This happens particularly with new students, or if we are over-stressed or over-worked. It's a product of not getting enough rest time, and Reiki helps to give us the rest we need: "Oh boy, you need sleep – here you go!" This is fine, because if this is what we need, then this is what we need. But when we fall asleep, although people say, "You are still giving yourself Reiki / Reiki carries on," are we really getting the full benefit out of it?

If we aren't tuned into the sensations, we aren't aware of where our imbalances are or where Reiki is going deeper. Yes, it may still work even if we fall asleep, but we aren't fully cognisant and participatory in the session. Therefore, the Reiki trance gives us the best of both worlds: still aware, yet in an incredibly restful state.

It's curious because it is like a dream state. We are aware during the time it's happening of what we are seeing, thinking or experiencing, believing that we are fully cognisant, but as soon as we come to and fully awaken, the vision or experience dissipates. This is different to the visions that we see in our mind's eye during Reiki, which remains with us and that we continue to be aware of. These visions are held at our conscious level, whereas the trance state visions appear to happen at a much deeper level. Could we be entering the delta or theta brainwave state? I think this is possible, but to date, no research has been done on this.

The other consideration is that it may be to do with the response of our right brain: Chris Niebauer writes most excellently in his book *No Self, No Problem*, telling us that our left brain lists, analyses and makes connections on a logical basis. It's where the sense of "I" is housed. But the right brain is the part that sees the bigger picture and understands the whole (as opposed to the left brain that sees the small details). Because it can't verbalise, it "nudges" the left brain when it comprehends something that the left brain doesn't – this, he argues, is what happens when we call something *intuition*.

> *"It may be that right-brain consciousness is also what happens when one is 'in the zone.' … Being in the zone is very similar to what psychologist Mihaly Csikzentmihalyi has called flow, using this term to describe the experience that someone has while being totally absorbed in the doing of something. He defines flow as: 'Being completely involved in an activity for its own sake. The ego falls away. Time flies. Every action, movement and thought follows inevitably from the previous one…'"*
> (Niebauer, 2019), (Csikszentmihalyi, 2009)

Could it be, then, that the Reiki trance is switching off our left brain – our cataloguing, analysing, rationalising self, and allowing the right brain to have a go at being in the driving seat? I very much suspect that this is indeed the case – but without being wired up and having my brain waves measured, of course I can't assert this as true. However, it's an interesting possibility. Once again, all we have is just the experience. No need to label it or judge it … just appreciate the experience of it.

Part II: Delving deeper

10. A Question Of Healing: Expecting Too Much

"Before enlightenment, chop wood and carry water. After enlightenment, chop wood and carry water"

- *Zen saying*

"I cured epilepsy."
"Reiki can fix bipolar."
"I will heal you of alcoholism."

Such claims that Reiki has "fixed" or will "cure" a condition completely, whether physical or mental, is unlikely to be true.

Reiki augments the body's own healing abilities to repair and heal itself in the way that it needs. We as practitioners can't know what will happen for and with a person, so using absolute terms such as "will fix" or "can cure" should be avoided. Reiki *may* help with [any condition]; *Reiki has been known to aid* [said condition]. Reiki may certainly have a positive and mitigating effect on [any condition] – *but we can't guarantee this every time, for every person.*

We are not dealing with something solid and tangible that can be measured in test results again and again. Reiki is ephemeral and individual.

The closest analogy is to meditation … a moving meditation that we can do for ourselves as well as for others. How does meditation work? Does

A Question of Reiki

it instantly and immediately remove all your guilt, fear, anger, anxiety, stress? Unless you have been practising for many years and dedicate yourself to the practice daily, then the answer is no. Continual meditation will help to ease our underlying issues, whether physical or mental, and improve the state of our mind, helping to move us into a more positive mental framework.

Reiki works in the same way. Yes, it *is* amazing. Yes, it can feel like magic, having this ability to make people feel better literally in the palm of our hands. Yes, it does work. But no, it is *not* a miracle cure! To expect to fix or cure every condition and every person is to expect too much of Reiki, and of ourselves. Remember: *there are no shortcuts*. Time, patience and practice.

The problem is this: that seeming miracles do appear to occur with Reiki. I have heard first-hand stories of miracle healings, of a serious issue being cleared up in just one or a handful of sessions. I have experienced it as well, for myself and for friends and clients.

A "healing crisis" is when a receiver of Reiki becomes extremely ill after the session, feeling as though they have flu-like symptoms, or a rash appears with a headache or stomach ache, or they have a crying fit that lasts for longer than usual. Yet after several hours or perhaps a day, they feel well again – all of these symptoms have passed. This is the manifestation of releasing what has been stored in our body and is no longer needed – it's clearing out the "gunk" that we have held inside, and we feel so much better after this: lighter and clearer, almost like a new version of ourselves.

This is one type of miracle. Others are physical issues being cleared up in one or a handful of sessions, or it may even be that a condition someone has been dealing with for months or even years is suddenly healed. However, in just over sixteen years, the number of miracles that I have seen and experienced has been fewer than I can count on both hands. These are called miracles because that is exactly what they are: something extraordinary, unusual and not normally occurring. To expect miracles all the time is to disappoint yourself and, more dangerously, your recipient.

Tadao Yamaguchi says that members of his own family were cured of tuberculosis with Reiki:

> *"He [Mr Sugano] gave her intensive treatments and she was privileged also to receive treatments from Hayashi Sensei himself. Thanks to this attention she made a complete recovery from TB, which at the time was thought to be incurable."*
>
> (Yamaguchi and Petter, 2008)

He then goes on to say that his own uncle also completely recovered from tuberculosis through Reiki treatments. This is amazing, and it sounds like a miracle. Most people would expect Reiki treatments to amount to a few hours per week at most, but Yamaguchi's story highlights the fact that prolonged, intensive and regular treatments may be able to produce near miraculous results. We shouldn't be discouraged if we don't see immediate results; persistence may be the answer to healing stubborn conditions and ailments.

Miracles and amazing healings *can* occur with Reiki, but we can't guarantee them, nor expect them, nor that a positive healing effect for one client *will* be repeated with another. Reiki can help us to deal with all sorts of conditions, over a number of sessions and a period of time. It can help us to get to a better place mentally and physically, but it is the promising of definitive results as a blanket statement that we should be wary of.

Some years ago, my partner suffered from low back pain, with very painful flare-ups. He had been suffering with this for a number of years. We conducted a Reiki session, and I focused solely on that area of pain. As I sat there, my hands gently warming up and increasing in heat, I suddenly saw in my mind's eye Reiki as a grid of white lines of energy, against a backdrop of black (which I perceived as space, or the void). I gently mused to myself, *Well, if Reiki is constant and infinite, why can't I bring as much as is needed to completely heal him?* Lo and behold, there was a surge through me, a feeling of what I can only describe as "blossoming", and energy just flowed and flowed and flowed …

"What the heck did you just do?!" cried my partner, also feeling this incredible energy and not sure what to make of the strange and sudden sensations.

"I don't know!" I said. "I just … wondered about the infinite Reiki!"

After that, my partner never experienced that back pain again. Years of on-and-off suffering had been fixed in that one session, much to our wonder. I didn't control it. I didn't "do" anything, except receive a vision. I didn't expect a miracle, but one happened. Yet I have never been able to replicate that vision, that incredible connection, or that type of healing since, not with my partner and with anyone else, despite seeing clients with the same kind of problem. I think this perfectly illustrates that "Reiki is Reiki" outside of our personal desires and expectations!

On the flip side of this, I have seen clients for other types of physical conditions, who I thought that I would be able to help in on-going sessions, yet they stopped coming to me after four, five or six treatments, because their condition or pain wasn't being helped or healed in the way that they hoped or expected that it would. Perhaps further treatments would have helped, or perhaps I wasn't the right Reiki practitioner for them … who can say? Perhaps Reiki as a treatment wasn't right for them at this time. Again, this is something that is outside of my own control and shows that I as the healer can't make expectations or guarantees: I can only do what I can do, offering Reiki and allowing the client, or the recipient, to receive that energy.

What can we expect with Reiki?

The true answer to this question is:

- Don't expect anything!
- No judgements, no attachments, no expectations!

Although these statements are true, I understand that they aren't very satisfying. They don't tell us how Reiki may be able to help ourselves and others, which is the real question.

As a general rule, the milder the issue, the greater the chance that Reiki can help in a single session.

- Headache? Reiki
- Tired eyes or feet? Reiki
- Got a cold? Reiki
- Slightly stressed? Reiki
- Someone made you angry? Reiki
- Fallen over and got a bruise or abrasion? Reiki
- Stomach ache? Reiki
- Struggling to sleep? Reiki

Reiki, Reiki, Reiki!

Reiki can generally help things we would perhaps term as "one-offs", immediately and fully, in a single session. With the common cold, I have found that although Reiki won't make it completely disappear in a single session, it can help to lessen the sore throat and blocked sinuses. It can also help the recovery in a quicker time frame.

The only mild thing that Reiki won't help with consistently, I have found, is tiredness or headaches caused by dehydration. Most people don't drink enough water, and our body suffers. We may not be aware of the signals our body is sending us, because we don't always pay full attention to ourselves. If you have a headache and Reiki doesn't shift it, drink water and then drink more water.

The more serious or long-standing a health issue or problem is, the more sessions it's going to take to help. Again, I would never say that, even in the long term, Reiki is going to "fix" a medical condition. That is very unlikely. Reiki *may* help to ease and minimise symptoms of various conditions. This effect is accumulative; the more Reiki you experience, the more effect and benefit it will have. Once again, we can directly compare this with meditation: the more we practise meditation, the more we notice a difference within ourselves, beginning to change in a positive way. But if we give up after the first try, because we "can't turn our brains off", we will never get to the point where meditation makes a noticeable difference.

Similarly, Reiki has a progressive effect that increases with ongoing sessions. This is why healers should, ideally, be practising Reiki daily, or at least several times a week. Regular Reiki helps us to remain balanced, centred and calm, as well as peeling away the outer layers of our problems, beginning to heal from the inside at deeper levels. Our fears, guilt, anger and anxieties are gently (or profoundly) unpacked so that, rather than storing them, we can release them and let them go, clearing our past and assumptions to move forward. I am of course talking here about our mental and emotional experiences that may need healing. Physical problems may come from the same root, though: what manifests as a physical issue may, at least in part, have its roots in mental or emotional stress.

We now know from studies that stress is not just "in your head and you need to relax". When left unchecked, stress causes physical disturbances in the body, such as back pain, chest pain and even heart problems. It can weaken the immune system, leaving us more susceptible to illnesses. Therefore, what manifests physically may need dealing with emotionally and mentally. Reiki can help us not only get to the symptoms, but also to the root cause of a problem. By healing the underlying issue – in this case, what has caused the stress – the person can begin to heal physically. This is one of the reasons why we should be doing a full-body Reiki treatment for ourselves and others. It's also good for a healer to have Reiki from another healer, as the experience is different to self-Reiki and can be incredibly beneficial.

We may not always know what the issues are that need healing. Indeed, the client may not themselves know the root cause of their issues, but a full treatment covers the whole body, all main organs, as well as each of the energy centres. So whichever part of the body is effected by the symptoms *and the root cause* will be covered with a full session, whether we or the client know about it or not. In this case, the person who comes to you complaining of back pain and constant tiredness may not even realise they are stressed. Through the course of one, two or three Reiki sessions, once the physical pains have been lifted, they may come to realise that something else is wrong. They may then start to reflect on this and notice other symptoms or emotional issues. Further Reiki sessions then start to balance the emotional disturbance, and the person may come to realise what in their life is off kilter, or not working for them.

I see Reiki healing like an onion: peeling back one layer after another, until we reach the core of the issue. This may happen quickly, or it may be a slow gradual process as the person gains insights into one problem and starts dealing with that issue in their own way and at their own pace. Once one problem is seen and healed or dealt with, we may discover a deeper issue and start working on that, and so on. From this example, we can see that the deeper or more long-standing an issue is, the more sessions it may take to gently peel away at layers, and to fully recover and heal.

With long-standing physical issues, while Reiki may not be able to fully heal a person, it can help to ease the physical symptoms: the aches and pains. It can also – and this is just as important – help someone to deal with their condition on a mental and emotional level, for them to come to a place of acceptance in their minds. It can help a person to grow and be comfortable in themselves *with and beyond their current condition*. In other words, healing into wholeness, as opposed to healing to make better.

Let us take cancer as an example. At the extreme, if someone is terminally ill, no amount of Reiki is going to miraculously heal them, but it can help to minimise the physical pain. It can also help someone to come to terms with their condition and their imminent death. It can help to soothe the emotions and the mind, bringing a sense of calm and peace. The state of mental well-being is actually good for the physical body too, as a calm peaceful mind helps to minimise the pain that we experience.

Death isn't something that is talked about in our society; it's treated like a taboo. Most of us don't see death; we don't talk about it openly. As a consequence, many of us are fearful of death, and even of thinking about it. Death is inevitable for all of us. We can't escape it, so we shouldn't fear it – fear only prevents us from enjoying our life. If we can help someone to accept death, to come to terms with it, we are helping them to make peace within themselves, in their mind, body and soul. We are, through Reiki, helping to take away the fear.

Someone who has cancer but isn't terminally ill will benefit in the same way from Reiki: an easing of the physical pain and helping the mental and emotional state, retaining a sense of calm and clarity. Reiki may well assist with the effects from medical treatments such as chemotherapy. Remember that Reiki is a *complementary therapy*: it can work alongside any other treatments and medicines, *but it can't and shouldn't replace them*. Reiki is now used in many countries as a complementary therapy alongside cancer treatments, in hospices and hospitals, and in personal settings.

The more serious a condition, the more Reiki sessions will be required: a cancer patient would ideally have Reiki at least twice a day, every day. However, that isn't easy and certainly not if someone is paying a practitioner, as obviously that would become expensive. But giving Reiki to a friend or on a voluntary basis, as often as possible, is going to see much more of an impact than a one-hour session once or twice a week.

We can't fix epilepsy with Reiki (yes, someone once asked me this). Ongoing Reiki may help to minimise epileptic fits and it *may* help to calm the episodes, but unless a miracle occurs, it won't fix it. As mentioned earlier, this is true of any medical condition. What happens for a person with a particular condition is going to be as individual as they are. Ongoing sessions along with discussions with that person, how they feel and what they notice, is your guideline, along with experience and practice.

When someone asks me if Reiki "will fix" their [insert condition here], I tell them something along these lines:

"That isn't how Reiki works. Reiki is an energy-based practice that works with you, on an individual basis, helping to balance and align what you may need on any or all levels – physically, mentally, emotionally, and even spiritually. I can never make any guarantees with Reiki because it's what you take from the healing. It may help to minimise any symptoms or to reduce episodes of pain and the strength of the pain, but it isn't a miracle cure. Everyone is different, so has a different experience with Reiki. Most people find that it's very relaxing, that it helps to reduce stress and to bring the mind into a calm and clear place, and that physical pain is reduced. You may find more profound effects than that in the days after the session, but that will be dependent upon your individual experience."

Most people are absolutely fine with this explanation and completely understand. They also appreciate that more than one session may well be needed, particularly for an underlying or ongoing illness or condition. People who would like a Reiki session would much rather that we, the healers, are completely honest with them, than try to make more of Reiki than can be expected or guaranteed.

Reiki has helped with conditions such as fibromyalgia and chronic fatigue syndrome. It has helped with arthritis and chronic back pain. I have had students come to learn Reiki because they or a family member suffer from these conditions. The benefit of Reiki to their lives has been a constant source of help and comfort to them. With these kinds of conditions, we can't say that the person will be cured, but they will become more balanced within themselves, perhaps experience less pain and feel more in control. Reiki is "calm mind, calm body". It isn't a miracle: it's acceptance of what *is*. In other words, *healing into wholeness*.

Help for psychological and mental health issues is going to be determined by the complexity, severity and underlying state of the individual. Bipolar disorder, for example, can't be "fixed". However, Reiki may help someone deal with their psychological state, and it may help them emotionally. It may, after months or even years, help to minimise the symptoms. There are varying complex factors involved around these (and similar) conditions.

The measurement for mental health is different than that for a physical condition, such as, for example, a broken leg. It can be subjective – "what is your mood score today?" – or more complex as doctors and mental health workers assess individuals, as well as the ongoing emotional impacts and current life circumstances. Reiki may help a condition such as bipolar disorder by minimising the triggers and evening out the bumps. Everyone with a mental health condition will have their own emotional needs and past issues that interrelate with that condition, including possible trauma.

Working on healing past issues or someone's sense of identity or emotional stress may be a great help in releasing some of the pain that the person experiences emotionally. But in no circumstances should we ever say that we can or will "fix" someone. Reiki treatments may certainly help someone on their ongoing life journey, bringing peace, calm and physical ease.

If a miracle does occur – fantastic! Celebrate it, be awed by it, be humbled by it. But don't expect that miracle to repeat itself. Remember: no attachments, no expectations. Just – Reiki.

When to stop doing Reiki

What if your client or recipient isn't getting anything out of the Reiki sessions? What if they are not seeing any results – or don't feel that there is enough progress? I have seen people panicking on social media, thinking that they are a failure as a healer, because their recipient "didn't feel anything". A person who doesn't feel anything during the treatment doesn't have anything to worry about – we explored this earlier, in chapter 8: they may experience shifts physically or mentally afterwards, in the following few days or weeks, because Reiki is about bringing healing, which can take some time to manifest, shift and clear.

But what if they have had several sessions and are still not feeling anything at all? What do we do? Or what if we, as the healer, don't see any progression in the client – if they keep coming back but are talking about the same issues; the same level of anxiety or fear; the same pain; or their condition is getting worse?

First of all, *there is no failure!* The only failure is if we don't put the needs of our client front and centre, and we are not being honest, dedicated and diligent with our practice of Reiki. If nothing seems to be working for that client, we need to explore why. One possibility is that something is happening, but it's subtle and gentle, occurring at a deeper level and not at the surface or in a profound way. Obviously, this is difficult to point if either we or the recipient can't see the result, but perhaps we can help by asking certain questions about their life, condition or state of mind, or even ask them to write a diary of their experiences and how they feel. Perhaps the exploratory discussion or the diary will reveal something otherwise hidden.

If this isn't the case, and we really don't feel that the client is getting any benefit at all, it may be time to consider other options. As a general guideline, I would be exploring further help if there hasn't been any improvement after six treatments at the most. I would expect to see some improvement by this point, or have the client tell me that they feel better in some way. This doesn't mean completely healed, but if nothing at all has changed for the client by now, we need to look at why. Perhaps the client needs more substantial help, in the form of counselling or medical treatment. We need to consider the client's health first, not our ego of "I and only I can help this person". We may need to consider suggesting alternative sources of help for a client, or making a referral to a counselling service or to their doctor.

If the client has an addiction problem that they felt was under control and they came for Reiki as a non-didactic way to treat it but are not seeing any results, we should consider advising them to seek addiction recovery help.

I reiterate that suggesting or referring to other specialists isn't a failure. We can't know how Reiki may help an individual, and if it seems that someone isn't getting better under our care, we serve our clients in the best way by doing what is right for them.

The reverse is also true. Sometimes people are referred to Reiki as a treatment by friends or other holistic services as a way to help them manage their illness, condition or issue. It's often the case that Reiki is, indeed, a beneficial treatment, but sometimes another service may be best for them at that time. It may be that once they are receiving counselling, medical care or addiction recovery treatment, then Reiki *alongside* that treatment helps their healing process. An individual is usually going to be thankful if you are being honest and help them to find the right treatment for them.

Summary

- Don't expect miracles with Reiki.
- Miracles can occur but can't be guaranteed – these are few and far between.
- Reiki works with the individual being treated, so the outcome may

be different each time.
- The more serious or long-standing an issue, whether physical or mental, the more Reiki sessions will be needed.
- Reiki isn't likely to fix or cure, but it may help to minimise symptoms and help with feelings of mental well-being.
- Reiki can help to get to the root cause of an issue, healing what needs to be healed on all levels.
- There may be times when Reiki doesn't seem to be helping a condition, and in this case we should be honest and consider suggesting or referring the recipient for appropriate help, such as counselling or seeing their doctor.

11. Reiki Goes Where It Needs To – So Why The Hand Positions?

"For it is in the giving that we receive"

- St. Francis of Assissi

"Reiki goes where it needs to go."
"Reiki is intelligent."
"Just put your hands anywhere – Reiki will find a way."
"Ten minutes is enough; you don't need a whole hour."

If Reiki, as energy, goes wherever it's needed in a person, why do we bother with specific hand positions? Why cover all of the body, front and (sometimes but not always) back? Why not just keep our hands in one position through the whole session, allowing the energy to zip around and cover everything itself?

There are some types of spiritual and energy healers outside of Reiki practice who work in this way – they don't move their hands, instead remaining in just one position through the whole process, so it's a valid healing method. There are, however, reasons why we move our hands around the body within the system of Reiki.

The Reiki hand positions

In traditional Western Usui Reiki, we use particular hand placement positions when treating another person. If you are unfamiliar with these hand positions, they are as follows:

1. Start at the head. Fingertips placed on the forehead; hands resting gently on the head. (Alternative: palms gently cupped over the eyes).
   1a. Follow first position by one hand at either temple (side of the forehead).
2. Back of the head.
3. Cupping sides of the face, on the cheeks.

Note: the reason that we start at the head is that this helps to calm and relax the mind. Our minds are busy and restless, often distracting us, asking questions and casting doubts. By beginning our session at the head, we can help to bring the mind to a place of quiet and calm, which then helps to relax the body in turn. We can also place our hands on the shoulders (one hand on each shoulder) at the beginning, before moving our hands to the head. This is a gentle way to start the session.

4. Hands at the throat position, held at the "V" of the throat (not too high up, to avoid choking the person).
5. Heart position. Here we can have our hands above and below the heart, avoiding the personal chest area, or hands off the body, above the heart.
6. The shoulder and wrist of each arm in turn, or alternatively, upper arm and then lower arm on each side.
7. Solar plexus – this is the centre of the lower ribs. Here we can have our hands placed one below and one above, or side by side, with the

fingers of one hand pointing at the wrist of the other, stretched across the body.

8. Sacral – Just below the navel, same as above: hands above and below each other, or stretched across side by side.

9. Root. The root area is located in the personal area of the genitals. Therefore our hands either need to be above this or at either side in parallel with the root, at the hip area. Alternatively, we can have both hands on one hip, and then swap to the other side of the body.

10. Hip – knee – ankle of each leg in turn. Alternatively, both hips, one hand on either, both knees and both ankles. Or, both hands cupped at each knee, holding the knee above and below, then cupping the ankle, doing each in turn on either side.

11. If we finish here, we complete the session by holding the feet, giving Reiki to both or to each in turn.

We may want to continue the session and ask our client or recipient to turn on their front so that we can Reiki the back:

12. Top of the spine, our hands coming across the shoulders with our fingertips meeting the wrist of the other hand.
13. Across the shoulder blades.
14. Across the mid back and lower ribs.
15. Across the lower back, covering the kidneys.
16. Knees and feet to finish.

These are the main areas and hand positions to cover. As you can see, these placements cover almost every area of the body and every major organ, as well as every major chakra (energy centre) point.

We don't always know the root cause of a client's issue; indeed, we may not know much about why they want a Reiki session, if they choose not to disclose that information. Sometimes, a person wants Reiki simply as a general "pick me up", or to help with a sense of re-balancing. Or for something deeper or more specific, they may tell us only that "It's an emotional issue" or "I'm feeling quite stressed". They may not want to tell us much at all, which is within their right. The client themselves may not know exactly what is wrong. They may know their symptoms, but what someone feels physically or emotionally may be a manifestation from an unidentified root cause.

If we only cover the areas where we think that an issue is causing physical, mental or emotional pain, we are not giving the client the greatest chance to heal at every level. What if the root cause is held at a different area than where the symptoms are manifesting? What if more underlying issues are held at various energy centres, or organs? We cover every area in a full treatment to give Reiki the chance to flow and to *focus* on each main point. It's a bit like taking an energy bath. If you were to take a physical bath, you wouldn't just dip your toe in the water and then say, "Well, that's me cleaned!" We put our whole selves into the bath to give our full body a good clean!

The focus of the hands on each position brings us to our next point…

Attention!

The key to the benefit of Reiki is intention. A person is helped in their healing process when we focus on them, when we bring our intention into the session. If a "sham practitioner" were to perform a Reiki session, placing their hands in the relevant positions and going through the motions, would a recipient receive the same benefit – the same healing effects?

No, they wouldn't – because the sham practitioner isn't stepping into the connection of universal *ki*; they are not bringing their intention and attention to the moment. So, while it's true that Reiki will indeed flow wherever it's needed, if we leave our hands in one place for a longer period of time, let us consider what happens when we place our hands at specific points with intention. We become aware of that area … we bring our *attention* to it. If someone places their hand on your shoulder, you are very immediately aware of the touch of their hand. You know how your shoulder feels under their hand: does it feel gentle, comforting? Or is there too much pressure? Does it feel uncomfortable? Our attention is immediately drawn to touch. So when, in Reiki, we place our hands on an area, both we as the healer and our recipient naturally bring our *attention and focus* to that specific place. Our *intention* is for Reiki to flow to this area, helping healing commence. We *specifically* focus here. By doing this over and over, everywhere, back and front, we give our focus and attention to as much of the body and the energy centres as possible. Again, it's exactly like the analogy of taking a bath: we are soothing and cleaning all over! When our attention and intention is focused, energy follows. We are mindful of this person, in this area, for healing. All of our attention is held in one place.

Our hands, as we have said, are our focal point with Reiki, so this is where we feel the energy flowing. (Some people also feel Reiki coming through their feet, making them feel fidgety or extra warm. This may be due to the fact that we also have chakra points at the balls of our feet as well as in the centre of our palms). By using our hands as focus tools, it helps us to concentrate on the feel of Reiki, of energy and of the healing taking place. It's often reassuring for a client who is laying with their eyes closed, and quite literally in your hands, to feel those hands gently resting on them. This can help to give them a sense of security, to know whereabouts you are as they lie there relaxing. The focus of feeling your hands on their tummy or arm, for example, helps to draw their attention to that area and become aware of anything that they may be feeling (this also helps to distract them from their busy minds!).

This is one reason why the hands-on approach can be better than the hands-off approach. Both are perfectly viable, but with the hands-on approach the client feels your touch and may gain a sense of security, comfort and focused attention. With the hands-off approach, the client may be wondering in their minds where you are hovering around them! They also won't have that same physical connection of touch, which can serve as reassurance. Reiki works just as well with hands-off, but it's the connection, the comfort, that may be lacking.

Some clients do prefer hands-off – perhaps they don't like being touched – so of course in these instances we must always accede to a client's preference. In traditional Japanese Reiki, Usui taught Reiki as a hands-*on* practice. It has become hands-off as it has developed down the cultural line. By all means, try both ways – hands-on and hands-off – and see which you prefer. But the point is that by covering each position, whether hands-on or hands-off, we give *focus* to every part of the body.

To back or not to back!

A full Reiki session will usually include turning your client or recipient over on to their front so that you can cover their back as well. However, not every healer does this, and it seems to be considered as less important than the front. This naturally depends on the situation at the time and the individual that we are with.

It can be beneficial to include the back positions because it feels complete. Front and back, every possible point covered, is completing the "energy bath". It feels lovely for the client, and of course Reiki is then also given to areas that can't be reached from the front. It's particularly important to have our hands on the back if the client has a physical back problem of any kind. Also, the top of the spine can be a good place to concentrate for conditions such as fibromyalgia or chronic fatigue syndrome, as the spine is connected to the central nervous system.

You may find, however, that during a session you have spent so much time on the front that you don't need to do the back. Or you may feel your recipient is so relaxed and comfortable that you don't want to turn them onto their front as this would disturb them. If they don't have a specific back condition, and you have spent a long time treating the front, it is absolutely fine to leave the session at that. In each case, use your judgement as to what you feel is required. There is a saying that "the front soaks through to the back", which means that the energy naturally moves from the front to the back as well. This is one reason why some healers feel they don't always need to cover the back of a person.

I have conducted a few Reiki sessions only on the back, either at the client's request or because it felt like the right thing to do at that time. It can be very relaxing. As it's not somewhere that people can reach for themselves, it can also feel very comforting. My personal experience has been that particularly the top of the spine, relating to the central nervous system, and the kidney area, where the adrenal glands are located, are important and beneficial positions to work on. As a Reiki healer, it's difficult to Reiki yourself on your back. Having another healer do this for you is much easier, and it can be a real treat!

With clients, I treat each session on its own merits rather than having a proscribed, methodical treatment. A formal session can last anywhere from 45 to 90 minutes, depending on how much Reiki a person needs, how long I feel I need to stay at each position, and whether to do the back or not. I often find that I have spent so long doing the front, that in a clinical setting where I have to be aware of time, there isn't enough time to do the back. If I have a client where it's important for back positions to be covered, I do ensure that I make the time to do this. Every session is different: be guided by your own experience, your client's needs and, of course, your intuition.

The Byosen technique

I have described above the traditional hand positions for Reiki. This is a modern Western method. The reason for it is, as I said, to cover every part of the body and every major chakra position. The other reason for this method is to help healers remember a *formula* for the Reiki treatment. It can be tricky to remember so much at the beginning of Reiki training, and the specific hand positions can be a helpful guide for new students.

The original method for Reiki treatments was known as *Byosen*, which has come to mean *scanning*. Although this isn't the literal translation of *Byosen*, it does describe the method. In *Byosen*, the head positions are covered first. After these, the healer would then simply place their hands on any area of the body that they knew needed treating – if there was a known physical issue – or they would "scan" the body, finding the energy and where healing was required, using their intuition.

With this method, the healer gently moves their hands a few inches above the body, scanning until they feel a sense of heat or a magnetic pull, indicating where healing is needed. When a sensation of some kind is felt, the healer places their hands at this position and stays here for as long as necessary, whether for 20 minutes, 30 minutes, or even the whole session. Once the sensations of heat or tingling calm down, the hands are then moved, scanning again and finding the next area to treat. In this way, it may be that only a handful of positions are covered during one session.

Byosen relies much more on intuition, yet it can be helpful to a student of Reiki to familiarise themselves with the sensitivity of energy. Some healers prefer this method, as they feel that being able to use their intuition is much more natural than the more proscribed Western hand positions. Some prefer the hand positions as it gives a signpost about what to do and where to go next. Both methods are fine, and most healers actually use a mixture of the two, basing their decision on what feels right for that particular session.

For example, we may feel that we know where to place our hands on a recipient, as we know the problem. We are happy to go through the proscribed hand positions, but during the session we feel intuitively that our hands want to go elsewhere: they may be drawn to a different area completely and may want to spend a lot longer in that area. Our intuition is rarely wrong! If our hands feel "magnetised" or start pulling of their own accord to an area, or become hot when hovering over a certain point, trust yourself and place your hands there.

By allowing ourselves to become aware of our sensitivity, we strengthen our intuition and our confidence in treating others with Reiki.

Time and position

Of course, we don't always have to do a full 45 to 90 minutes Reiki session. We may not have the time to do this, it may be an informal session for a friend or family, or your client or recipient may not want to sit still for that long. We *can* do a shorter session. Even 10 minutes can be remarkable and elicit some satisfying results. "Any Reiki is better than no Reiki" is an apt saying!

You will be surprised to discover what can be achieved in a shorter space of time. It's possible that the most heat felt, and the most dramatic shifts and sensations, are related to surface or physical healing, clearing the outer or more immediate issues first. More subtle sensations may be linked to deeper healing, on the mental or emotional layers, therefore potentially producing a longer-term impact.

The reason for the longer full session still stands – that we are giving the client the greatest chance of healing all over and at every level (remember the energy bath!). This also gives the client or recipient an opportunity to fully relax. How often do any of us ever get to take time out? This in itself is therapeutic; being able to fully relax triggers the relaxation response in the body. This is when our body is most effective at healing itself, which is why doctors tell ill patients to get some rest.

A full Reiki session has many benefits, including that it:

- helps the client to relax
- triggers the relaxation response

- heals on every level
- can help to boost the immune system

We can do shorter Reiki sessions when necessary and required. With shorter sessions, again we need to be guided by what feels right, because it may feel far too rushed to try and cover every area in a short space of time, so hand placements at just one or two positions may be better. If someone has a specific issue – arthritis in the knee, or a stinging cut, for example, then of course we can place our hands exactly where healing is needed – in this case, we don't have to go through a variety of positions.

Go with your instincts. What feels right to you? What does your intuition say? What is best for you or your recipient? Explore your Reiki and try different sessions in different ways. If something doesn't feel right, don't do that again. If something goes very well, great, keep doing it. Be open and aware of your experiences as you experience them. That is all we need with Reiki.

We can complete a Reiki session by lying down or sitting in a chair, either way is fine. Sitting may feel more comfortable when doing Reiki for ourselves or others. Lying down obviously helps with relaxation and is the most common way to perform Reiki in a professional setting, but it may not always be possible with "informal" Reiki, when we are at home with friends and family. If you don't have a Reiki bed (massage bed), trying to do Reiki on someone lying on the floor can be uncomfortable for your back. Or if they are on a bed, you may find it difficult to get around them and comfortably reach each position. Sitting in a dining chair or armchair may be a more suitable option. Again, go with what feels right. Explore and have fun!

One of the beautiful effects of Reiki is that as the person giving the session, we also *receive* Reiki. As we step into the connection with Reiki, we are a part of that connection, so we also receive the healing benefit, along with our client. It's often the case that after a healing session for another person, the healer themselves feels good, clear in mind and body and happier. Reiki doesn't drain us but uplifts us.

'Reiki is intelligent'

I am slightly puzzled by this phrase that gets bandied around, as I am not entirely sure what it means. So let us explore it. Words and phrases are useful for us to communicate with and understand one another, but they can also create certain assumptions. When we look at these phrases and start to break them down, we find that they don't actually convey the true meaning.

Let me give you an example by taking the word *Reiki*. We often say, "I do Reiki" or "I'm giving Reiki." But what does *Reiki* actually mean? *Reiki*: means universal *ki* / divine spiritual energy / spiritual life force energy.

In the above phrases, what happens if we replace the word *Reiki* with the meaning behind the word? "I do spiritual energy." "I'm giving divine spiritual energy."

Is this true? Does this make sense? How can we "do" or "give" something that is already there, all around us, within each of us? Suddenly the phrase doesn't make sense. It would be better to say: "I connect with Reiki [divine spiritual energy]" or "I work with Reiki [spiritual life force energy]."

Doesn't that make more sense? Of course we know what is meant when someone says "I do Reiki", but it isn't the *full true meaning*. We need to look behind the word Reiki to really understand the truth.

When we say *Reiki is intelligent*, what do we really mean by this? I think what people mean when they say this is: "Reiki flows, and goes where it's needed, without direction or requirement from healer or recipient."

Reiki Goes Where It Needs To - So Why The Hand Positions?

This statement, in and of itself, is indeed true. Reiki is the spiritual energy that is within and without; it is "balance". Reiki will go where it's needed – that is the whole point of the Reiki session!

Is Reiki intelligent? If Reiki is intelligent and goes where it's needed, what do we bring to the table? What do we, as the healers, actually *do*? If Reiki is already there, the life force energy that simply exists, why do we need to do anything?

We need to bring our focus to Reiki to allow ourselves and others to access this healing process, this balance. Our external distractions of busy lives, distracted minds and constant emotional pull blocks our innate connection with something that simply *is*, that is always there. This is why we bring our attention to Reiki, and why we use our hands to focus that attention, bringing Reiki to where it's needed.

Perhaps we could think of Reiki as a "field" instead of as energy. A field permeates all of space, much like gravity. Changes in the strength of a field between different points result in motion and flow, just as differences in air pressure drive the wind. We can think of Reiki in this way, as using our focus and intention to manipulate the field of universal *ki*.

The energy of Reiki is then driven by changes in the field; energy and the field mirror each other. Electricity in a circuit will always follow the most direct path, and this appears intelligent, but it's a result of the electric current being driven by a field. In the same manner, Reiki is flowing in accordance with the field of universal *ki*, and it's always drawn to where it's needed most.

Reiki can then be thought of as either energy, essence or a field that is imbued with intelligence *through us that are alive with Reiki*. When we connect with the one great Reiki, we *are* the mind of Reiki! This is what we mean when we talk about no separation, no duality: we are all part of the whole; we are all connected.

Summary

- In Reiki, we use hand positions to cover every area of the body and the energy centres. This helps us to get to the potential root cause of an issue as well the symptoms.
- Jikiden Reiki uses *Byosen*, which is scanning the body and using intuition to find areas for healing.
- We use our experience and intuition as a guide to determine the time and position for each session, and to treat every session on its own merits.

12. Energy Systems: The Tanden And The Chakras

"When you touch the celestial in your heart, you will realize that the beauty of your soul is so pure, so vast and so devastating that you have no option but to merge with it. You have no option but to feel the rhythm of the universe in the rhythm of your heart."

- *Amit Ray, Meditation: Insights and Inspirations*

Within Reiki practice, we look at two systems to understand our inner energy: the tanden system and the chakra system. The tanden appears simpler than the chakras, and it can be said to be more closely aligned with Reiki as it comes from the same place, Japan, so let us have a look at this system first.

The Japanese tanden system of energy

The Japanese tanden system of working with energy is based at three points in our body and spirit:

- the *hara*
- the heart
- the head

In many traditions, including some martial arts, the *hara*, which is located a little below the navel, is the focal point, as this is the centre where our energy is stored, where it goes to and comes from. I think of this like a banked fire: our energy; our glowing embers of warmth are always there. When we focus on energy work, we move those embers into a controlled dynamic fire. That fire expands through our body, through our whole system, literally energising us. Returning to the *hara* strengthens those embers. This is also where we connect with earth energy – that is, energy that comes to us from below, from the earth, helping us to remain connected, centred and grounded.

The heart energy is our emotional energy, and the mid-point where our lower (*hara*) and upper (heavenly) energies combine.

The head, combining the crown and third eye chakras, is the seat of heavenly energy or spiritual energy, helping us to remain open to the "greater out there", the oneness, our connection to all that is.

Concentrating on these three tandens, visualising our energy moving up and down, flowing to and through the head, heart and *hara*, also helps to connect us – our outer self – to our tandens' energy. We develop clearer awareness and strengthen our sensitivity to the balance and movement of our inner energy, and continued practice and focus in this way can aid our spiritual growth. This is what tai chi and qi gong movements are about – purifying as well as strengthening inner *ki*. It's said that masters of these forms can not only concentrate their own *ki*, but they can also manipulate the *ki* of others.

In China, the free flow of our inner energy is dependent on the meridians, which are the channels in the body that provide the flow of the energy. Acupuncture, as well as traditional Chinese medicine, are based on clearing these meridian channels. The meridians, tanden – also called "Tan Tien" or "Dan Tien" in Chinese – and the chakras are each a system or map of interpreting and understanding the subtle energy system.

Chakras

Chakras are energy centres throughout our entire body. The system originates from India, and the word *chakra* means *wheel* or *vortex*. Chakras are described as a ball, wheel or flower of energy located at particular points in our body. There are many minor chakras throughout the whole body, and seven major chakras that run through the centre line from head to foot. These are not physical, so we can't prove that they exist, but we can experience them, just as we feel the energy of Reiki.

Each energy centre is associated with a specific trait, linked to particular aspects of ourselves. When we are balanced and whole, our chakras are clear and working perfectly ... when we are ill, stressed or out of balance, we can redress this by working on our chakra point, our energy centres. We will go through the traits in more detail later.

The chakra system has become quite a common feature within Western Reiki. However, it wasn't taught by Mikao Usui, because it's from a different cultural background. The chakra system became incorporated with Reiki much later when, presumably, some student realised that the hand positions cover the same points as the chakra centres. As a result of the conflation of systems and methodologies, some traditional teachers to this day don't teach the chakra system in their Reiki training classes. Others, including myself, who were taught the chakra system, continue to include it.

I do so because understanding the energy centres in relation to healing with Reiki makes sense to me. In my own training classes, I do make it clear to my students that the chakra system is a later addition to Reiki and wasn't part of the original teachings. Therefore, it's up to each individual whether they wish to work with this addition, or not. Some students may choose to incorporate the chakra system, while others prefer not to. It depends on whether the framework, as well as the feel of the energy, makes sense to you in this way.

Within Reiki, it's really only the major chakras that we focus on, and these energy centres are like a linchpin that hold together our physical, mental and emotional components. The seven major chakras can be used within Reiki to understand the body's *ki* system in more detail. These are associated with a spectrum of physical, emotional and spiritual facets of our being, starting at the lowest chakra, which deals with our physical needs, up to the crown of the head, which concerns our connection with the divine. We can relate any complaints to one or more chakras on which we can focus Reiki treatment. The following table gives a brief outline of this:

Name	Location	Colour	Physical Aspect	Mental & Emotional Aspect
Crown	Top of the head	Purple / white	Brian, Mind	Openness, Spiritual Connection
Third Eye	Centre of the forehead	Purple	Eyes, Nose, Facial nerves, Sinuses	Creativity, Intuition, Inner Awareness
Throat	At the 'v' of the throat	Blue	Trachea, Throat, Leading down the the lungs	Communication, Emotional Expression, Truth
Heart	Centre of the chest	Green / Pink	Lungs, Heart, Chest	Love, Compassion, Self-love, Forgiveness
Solar Plexus	Centre of lower ribs / diaphragm	Yellow	Stomach, Small Intestines, Liver	Self-trust, Willpower, Motivation, Self-esteem
Sacral	Just below the navel	Orange	Womb, Large Intestines, Kidneys	Trust, Emotional balance, Trauma, Addiction
Root	At the genitals	Red	Bladder, Urethra, Genitals	Ground, Feeling Centred, safe, loved & secure

A Reiki healer will use these chakra meanings to gain an insight into why more heat and tingling might be happening at, say, the solar plexus area. Here we can see that in energy terms, this is associated with self-trust, self-esteem, self-worth, and such like. Strong sensations felt in this area, either by the client or in the healer's hands, could relate to physical issues, or indicate healing is needed on an mental or emotional level, or even all of them.

We can see from the chart that mental or emotional healing could mean that someone is suffering from low self-esteem or a lack of self-worth. For example, from my own experience with giving treatments and speaking with students and clients, it seems that anxiety and irritable bowel syndrome (IBS) are closely linked: people suffering from one often also suffer with the other. IBS is physical; anxiety is a mental state (although it often causes physical reactions as anxiety can be felt in the body). So if we can help our client (or student or ourselves) to heal from anxiety, it may be the case that the IBS also disappears.

Heat and tingling at the throat chakra could convey a truth not spoken, difficult conversations, or a person who finds it difficult to speak up for themselves or to communicate their own emotional needs. This can lead to or manifest as a sore throat, shyness, coughing or "harrumphing" quite a bit. If we can help someone to understand that they can speak their truth, that they can open up to their emotional expression, any related physical issues may also be cleared.

Most often, it can be a more complex situation than this. Although the chakras work independently, they are also intertwined; they work together. A mental or emotional issue is often held at several chakra points, or at worst, all of them. Stress, for example, may affect the crown chakra (openness, no or limited spiritual connection), third eye chakra (can't feel their intuition), heart chakra (criticises self instead of loves self), and root chakra (doesn't feel secure or balanced).

By working on a full-body session in a Reiki treatment, we help to balance and bring Reiki to every area, therefore helping to bring back into alignment every chakra point, which in turn can bring down the levels of stress. As stress also affects the body in a physical way, Reiki at every point will help to ease physical symptoms and switch the central nervous system to the relaxation response instead of the fight or flight response.

Depression is an example I use often in my classes. I focus a lot on the mental and emotional state, because if we aren't happy, calm and centred in our mind, we are going to be unbalanced and unhappy on the outside. Our actions, behaviours, thoughts and feelings all stem from our mind – our mental and emotional being. By looking after our inner self and cultivating happiness, peace and calm that permeates outwards to our actions, behaviour, interactions and the choices that we make in our daily lives. See chapter 15 for further details.

Incorporating chakra work can help to bring balance as well as healing from the inside out, and ongoing sessions can help us to go deeper into ourselves and to find our own balance, purpose and even happiness.

Overactive, under-active, depleted and blocked chakras

The chakras are sometimes described as being overactive or under-active, depleted or even blocked. There is also discussion on which direction the chakras spin or should be spinning as a ball of energy at each given area. I have seen contradictory information in books and on websites and social media. Some people declare that all chakras spin clockwise, while some ascertain that each spins in the opposite direction to the one above it, and so on. So how do we know? Well, we don't. How can we prove this? What difference does it make? It really doesn't. Why get hung up on this? Energy is energy ... How does the client feel through our session? How do they feel afterwards? Do they feel relaxed, calm, good? Is it going to help them to know if their chakra is spinning clockwise or anti-clockwise?

We also need to realise that the current chakra system is only one branch that became popularised some time ago, and that the whole system is more complex than the way in which most of us understand it today. Therefore, we can say that this is a way simply to *interpret* how we feel and understand energy.

To read a couple of websites or to take as gospel the word of one or two people doesn't make us an expert. Just because someone says something is true doesn't make it so. For the purposes of Reiki, it doesn't matter about spinning chakras and their direction, just what you and your client feel when giving Reiki.

Under-active and overactive chakras are a way of saying that an energy centre is out of balance, through having stored too much or not enough energy at that area. A solar plexus chakra, for example, is "overactive" when someone has too much confidence, seen as arrogance and pride. Someone who is very bubbly and can't help but talk may have an overactive throat chakra. Someone who is overemotional, temperamental and sensitive may have an overactive sacral chakra. A depletion of chakras is the opposite of all this – lack of self-esteem and self-worth at the solar plexus; an inability to communicate emotions at the throat; an inability to problem-solve and feel safe in life at the root. Of course, we do need to balance all of this, being aware of the holistic being of a person, and that such behaviours and attitudes may be an intrinsic characteristic or caused by psychological reasons. These are merely examples that can help us in our work *and may indicate* what is going on (but don't take my word for it).

Then there are what people term "blocked" chakras, which is a more severe form of under-activity or depletion … This is where people feel that they have no emotion whatsoever at this area: "I can't feel love, my heart chakra is blocked."

What do we do in this case? Well, the good news is that it isn't terminal! A blocked chakra simply means that we are really struggling in that area and more healing work needs doing.

"How do I know if someone has a blocked chakra?" is a question I often hear from students. Firstly, I advise caution – this is one of those areas that I think has become overused. It's almost fashionable to have a "blocked chakra", and again this is a symptom of this kind of work becoming popular. Is the chakra really blocked, or are you just feeling a bit down? Who told you your chakra was blocked? Why? Could it just be that we need to do some healing work, both in terms of a healer helping to heal and boost your system, and you, as the client, doing the work that you need to, in terms of self-examination and working through your fears, doubts, patterns or anger? I think we walk a fine line with "blocked" chakras. How do we know what a chakra is doing – under-active or overactive, depleted or blocked?

Time, patience ... practice, practice, practice!

This takes time. You are not necessarily going to get it on your first session ... or even your second, or your third! Like anything else that we learn and develop, understanding energy and the feel of energy is a skill that builds up the more we practise with it. Awareness and sensitivity to feeling energy and sensations gently strengthens with practice and with time. Work in the way that makes sense to you, not because of what someone else has said. If "blocked" chakras don't make sense to you, then think, feel and express the way that energy and the energy centres do make sense to you.

The best way to understand this is to work on yourself first and foremost. Don't rush this. Take time with self-Reiki (or having regular treatments from a practitioner) to understand the patterns of your own emotions and feelings, and the relationship with your energy and chakra centres. This will give you a good guide and understanding. From here, as a healer, work on people close to you – willing family and friends. Only move on to working with others once you feel comfortable and confident in the way that you understand energy.

To work with chakras or not

Inclusion of chakra work will most likely be based initially on whether our own Reiki master taught the system in their class. If they did teach it, but you can't get on with the idea, if it doesn't make sense to you, then it's fine to simply give Reiki without trying to interpret chakra information. As I say, this is a later addition to Reiki and wasn't part of Usui Sensei's teachings. If you weren't taught the chakra system but you come across it after your training and you are interested, you can research some more and begin to incorporate it into your own healings.

The chakra system is simply a tool within Reiki and energy healing; a way to interpret what we are feeling and sensing. It doesn't make us a better healer or a more effective healer. Only we, in our actions and connection with Reiki, can affect how good we are. By this, I mean the dedication and time we put into practising self-Reiki and meditations. It really does make a difference in our learning, understanding and development. The research that we do, such as reading a variety of books on the subject, can open up our perceptions, think in new ways and take on new ideas. Talking to others, having discussions, having healings from another for ourselves, and even joining a local Reiki share will help. The more we delve into the world of Reiki, the better we will be in terms of our understanding, and then being able to communicate effectively and genuinely help other people. Through thorough engagement, we will also discover which methods, systems and practices work for us, and how and where we feel comfortable in receiving Reiki healing, or our self-practice, and in healing others.

No one is asking us to be perfect as a Reiki healer, or to be an expert or even a saint in our own lives ... but taking the time to develop our practice and work on ourselves really can make a world of difference in gaining a richer, deeper understanding, and feeling more confident in our own practice – whether this is ourselves, informal Reiki or in professional practice.

Summary

- The tanden system is a Japanese system of mapping *ki* energy.
- There are three tandens: below the navel at the *hara*, at the heart and at the head.
- Chakras are energy centres held throughout our body; this system originated in India.
- The chakra energy system was a later addition to Reiki and not part of Mikao Usui's original training.
- Although there are many chakra centres throughout our body, Reiki focuses on the seven major chakras from head to foot.
- Each chakra has a relationship with a physical area and a mental and emotional trait.
- By healing the chakras, we can help to heal physically, emotionally and mentally, and know where we may be out of balance.
- Chakras can be overactive, under-active, depleted or blocked.
- Learning what happens with the energy centres and how balanced or unbalanced they are takes time, patience, and practice, practice, practice!
- We don't need to work with the chakra system if it isn't something that we feel comfortable with. Traditional Reiki teachers still don't teach it in their classes today.
- Trust your own instincts and work in the way that feels right for you – not because someone has stated something as fact in a book, website or social media post.
- Take the time to work on yourself (and on willing family and friends) first and see how you feel in relation to your chakra centres.

13. Starting With A Strong Base

"The stillness in stillness is not the real stillness; only when there is stillness in movement does the universal rhythm manifest."

- *Bruce Lee*

A strong foundation is the core of everything. The base of a mountain; the roots of a tree; the foundations of a house – and us. We are exactly the same. A strong base helps us to withstand physical and emotional storms.

Many people have the idea that to be truly spiritual or gifted, we have to focus on the upper centres of the self – namely, the third eye and the crown chakras. While these can help us to deepen our intuition, connection and spiritual awareness, on their own they can't give us physical, mental and emotional strength. Our foundation – our base – is the *hara*, the lower tanden.

It may feel good to be "spiritual" and to be "high" on the spiritual plane, but we have to accept that we are physical beings too, living in the material world, experiencing everyday life and all of the problems within it. To deal with these problems, to be sure of our own self and to feel confident in knowing we can get through any issue, we must have a solid foundation. This is why we should spend just as much time, if not more, focusing on our lower body, lower energy centres and breathing. In fact, this is where we should start our practice, through Reiki and with meditation, and slowly, patiently, work our way upwards.

We can work on all of our chakras at the same time. We don't have to go through them one by one, but it's good to focus on the lower ones as much as – if not more – than the higher chakras, to maintain inner balance. This has the effect of creating stability and groundedness – literally feeling connected to our body and having our feet on the ground, as opposed to being in our mind, wandering here there and everywhere.

In terms of chakras or energy points, this base within us is located between the root and sacral chakra. As we breathe in, we take our breath down below our navel, and as we breathe out, we breathe up from this area. Try this for a few minutes and see what effect this has for you. What happens when we centre here? For a start, we become grounded. We become aware of our body, our self, our presence ... we come *back to the present, the here and now*. We stop flying around in our minds to the past or the future, or vague wanderings and daydreaming. How many of us are truly constantly *aware* of where we are, and when we are? Of being fully focused on our present surroundings and attention and feelings? Most of us are often off somewhere in our minds. This is why at a later point our recall about that particular time may be poor, because we were not *fully present*.

Being fully present brings us in to our centre, where we are in control of our whole self, mentally, physically and emotionally. When we are at our centre, we can deal with problems, verbal conflict and our own mind. This is why it's so important to know and remain at your centre.

Some people seem to believe that the lower energy centres are pretty much irrelevant, and therefore don't need much attention paid to them. The goal is to fully open up and align the upper chakras – but we only need to look at the chart in the chapter on chakras to see that even this idea isn't true. The two lower chakras, the root and the sacral, are incredibly important. The root represents stability and a sense of security and safety. The sacral is emotional balance, letting go of the past and dealing with our emotional issues. So even when looking at ourselves and our energy work from a chakra perspective, it makes no sense to ignore the foundations – quite literally, our physical and emotional stability!

Maslow's hierarchy of needs

We can also see this idea in terms of Maslow's *hierarchy of needs*. Abraham Maslow, an American psychologist (1908–1970), created an illustrative pyramid, showing a theoretical proposal on how people function.

As we can see from this pyramid (illustration overleaf), our sense of security, safety and basic needs are the foundation for everything that comes afterwards as we climb this pyramid. We can't reach the top with self-fulfilling satisfaction unless we have everything we need at the bottom of the pyramid – at our foundation. Our emotional well-being is dependent upon our physical well-being, and our physical well-being is dependent on having our basic needs met. You can see that Maslow includes well-being under *safety*, and then follows with *love*: feeling loved, feeling supported, feeling that we belong. As social creatures, even if we identify ourselves as "loners" or "non-sociable", we still need love and care – we literally can't thrive without it. Studies show that children who don't receive due care and love, who are not touched or hugged, have parts of their brains underdeveloped – their brains don't grow.

In her article The lasting impact of neglect, Kirsten Weir cites the case of The Bucharest Project (Humphreys et al., 2017), which studied young children in a Bucharest orphanage:

> *"Institutionalized children had delays in cognitive function, motor development and language. They showed deficits in socio-emotional behaviors and experienced more psychiatric disorders. They also showed changes in the patterns of electrical activity in their brains, as measured by EEG."*
> (Weir, 2014)

Illustration of Maslow's hierarchy of needs.

Transcendence — Highest, most inclusive and holistic level of consciousness characterised by spirituality and altruism

Self Actualisation — Achieving one's full potential, artistic pursuits, creativity, morality and spontaneity

Esteem — Respect, self-esteem, independence, mastery, status, prestige

Love & Belonging — Friendships, relationships, intimacy, affiliation, family and sense of connection

Safety — Personal security, emotional security, prosperity, stability, employment, health

Biology & Physiology — Air, water, food, shelter, sleep, clothing and warmth

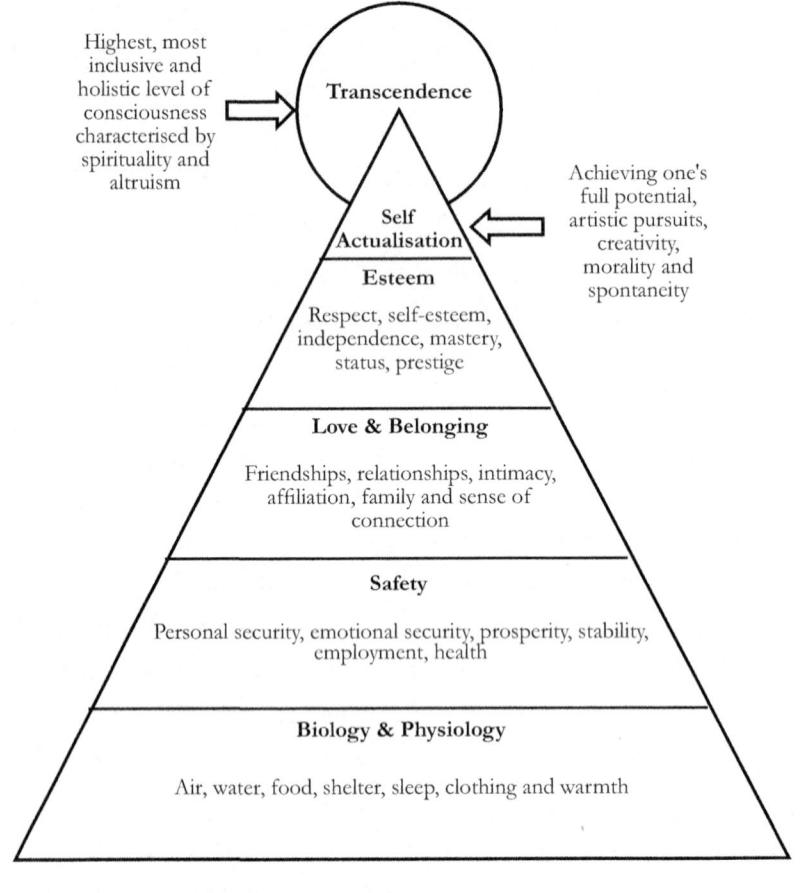

Illustration of Maslow's hierarchy of needs.

However, they also discovered that for children who moved to foster care prior to the age of two:

"…by age 8 their brains' electrical activity looked no different from that of community controls."

So the good news is that those same children, taken into a loving family, who are shown and given touch and emotional love, begin to develop and their brains grow in the normal way, making up for that lost development. The amount of love that we receive – or don't receive – has a very real effect on the growth and elasticity of our physical brain. This shows that feeling supported, sheltered and safe, and having our needs met, is absolutely fundamental to our personal development and growth on all levels.

Staying centred

Starting at our base creates the strong foundation that we can build from. Even if we put the idea of chakras to one side, we can look at our breath … What happens when we breathe down to the *hara*, below the navel? Most of the time we breathe shallowly, from our upper bodies. What happens when we take it deeper? We slow down and take better breaths. It's better for our whole body. If this is the place we should be breathing from, then it's an indication that this space within us is important! When we focus on our *hara*, we become more aware of our self, and we become more aware of our present … In other words, we become *fully engaged* in our life *as it is happening now*. We feel more real.

Dealing with issues isn't always easy: even if we are centred, we can still feel as though we have been thrown a curve ball, finding situations stressful or emotional. But when we are centred, even if we feel angry or need to have a cry, or feel our stress levels rising – *we are still able to get through this and see the issue objectively*. If we are not centred in ourselves when a problem arises, it's all too easy to go to pieces and not be able to see a way through. Depending on our own individual coping mechanisms, we may throw a tantrum, cry bucketfuls, overeat, or turn to drink or drugs. But when we are centred, we are less likely to go to our negative habitual coping mechanisms and are more likely to simply have a bit of a huff, let that stress out, and then deal with whatever it is that needs dealing with.

This is ultimately what staying centred is all about: being able to see and accept things as they are, whatever they are, without the need to wish them otherwise. It isn't always easy to be centred, and this is why we need to work at it, to put in the practice and time to help ourselves come to that place of strength – to *know* our centre and what it feels like. If, after a self-Reiki, you feel grounded, aware of yourself, aware of your whole body and clear in your mind, this is centredness. Imagine if you were this focused *all the time*! How amazing would that be? There are very few people who can remain centred and fully present 100 per cent of the time – but we can always work to become *more* centred, more *aware*.

A strong base is where we should always start from. It helps us in our practice of Reiki too. It helps us to grow upwards … like a tree, stretching up from its roots, growing its branches up and outwards. The wind comes along and shakes those branches, but the roots keep it strong and stable. We are exactly like the tree; if we haven't strengthened our roots, our base, we may easily give up with our energy work, or not know how to deal with any healing issues and difficulties that may arise. Our base is our energy core: it's the place our energy starts from and comes back to. Therefore, without taking the time to know it and understand it, our energy may be a weak flame, unable to grow to its full potential and unable to withstand the storm.

Practices to strengthen your foundation

Below are some basic exercises for you to try, to help focus on and strengthen your foundation:

- Practise being fully present in the present moment, wholly aware of what you are doing, whether that is sitting, driving, washing up, having a conversation or meditating. Set yourself a time limit of 10 or 15 minutes. Make a note, mental or on paper, every time within those 10 to 15 minutes whenever you notice your mind has wandered off, thinking of the past or future or daydreaming – when it isn't wholly engaged in what is happening right now. Check the count after the time is up. Does the result surprise you? You can extend this exercise by trying it daily and seeing if the results change over a period of a week or more.

- Practise breathing down to your *hara*. It's beneficial for your out breath to be longer than your in breath; for example, count in for four and breathe out for seven. Make this breath-to-*hara* practice part of your daily routine, with any other exercise or energy work that you do. Notice how you feel afterwards.
- While sitting, let your attention *really* focus on your whole physical being: the feel of what you are sitting on, how every part of your body feels, any discomfort, the sounds around you, what you can see … Really focus on your *present moment of being*.
- Place your hands on your tummy, with your navel at the centre. Your hands should be in a diamond shape, fingers pointing downwards. As you breathe, focus on your hands, on where they are, how it feels, and your breath as you breathe. See how you feel afterwards.

Keeping your attention absolutely focused is incredibly difficult, and even keeping full awareness for 20 seconds can be an achievement! Continual practice is the key to training your brain and developing the focus of your attention – so don't give up! The value of the practice is actually in the trying of it, not in the results. Every time you do these exercises you are strengthening yourself and your development.

Summary

- We must have a strong foundation from which to work within ourselves.
- This foundation, or base, is seated just below our navel, at our *hara*.
- This is both our physical and our energetic centre.
- A strong foundation helps us to grow and remain strong from within.
- A strong foundation helps us to: remain present; have clarity of mind; be able to deal with difficult issues more easily; accept what is; grow our energy as well as our practice of Reiki.

Part III: Practical Reiki

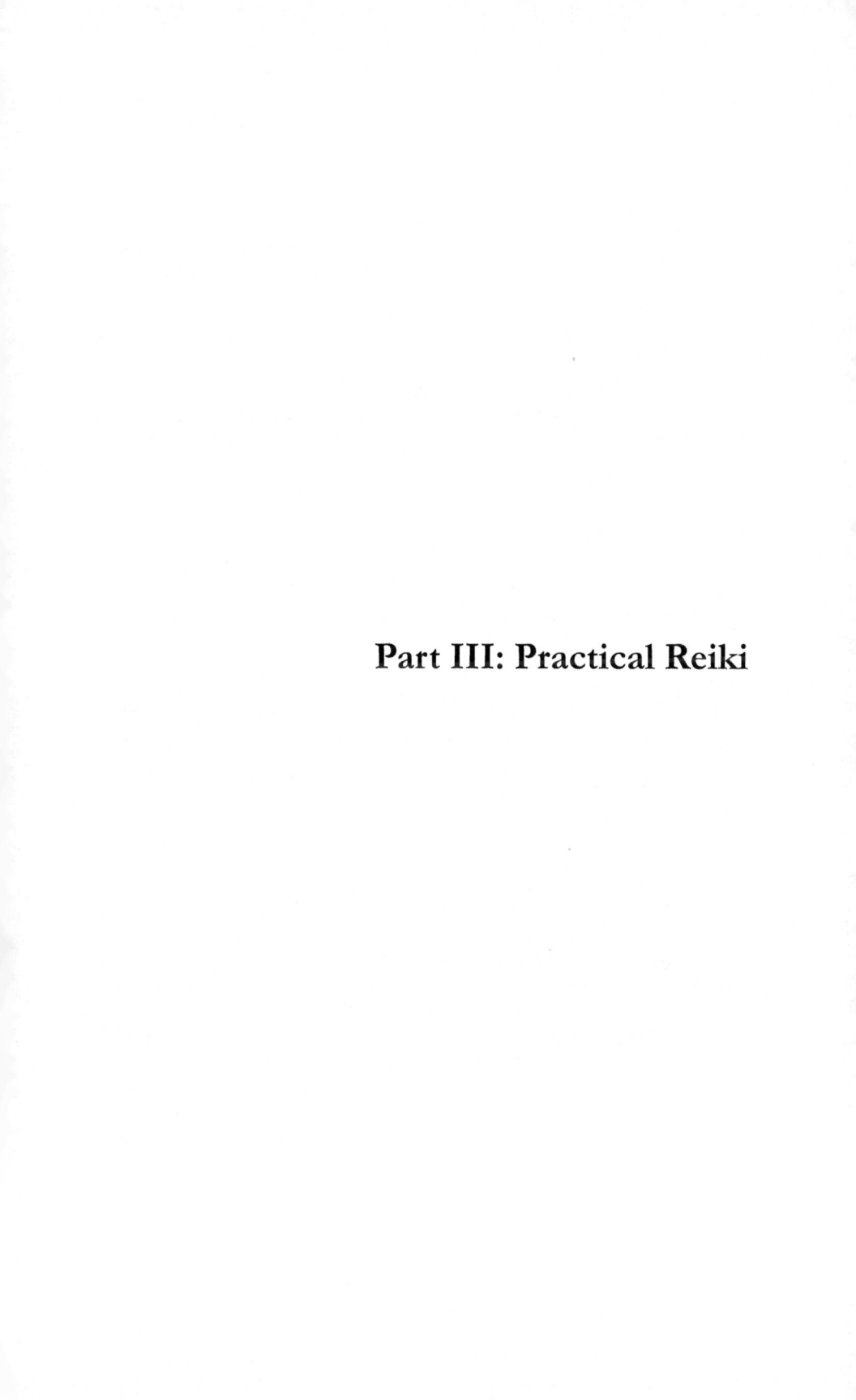

14. The Nature Of Reiki And Nature Reiki

> "Our task must be to free ourselves ... by widening our circle of compassion to embrace all living creatures and the whole of nature and its beauty."
>
> - *Albert Einstein*

Usui Sensei said that Reiki is the great universal energy that runs through every living thing. That includes us human beings, animals, trees, plants and the earth. Everything that is alive has *ki* and has Reiki.

According to this explanation, when we receive the Reiki *Reiju* (also known as the attunement or the initiation), we aren't given Reiki. It isn't a new gift that the master transfers to us. We already have Reiki; it's *already* within us. Let us explore this idea of the *Reiju* within the system of Reiki.

The Reiju and the one great Reiki

What happens when we have the *Reiju*? The master helps to hold the spiritual space for us so that we can open up and realise our own connection with Reiki: the master creates the conditions through their own focus and spiritual connection, to allow us to connect with our own Reiki, the oneness.

The process of *Reiju* is still, to this day, a fascinating one. The explanation that I have given above is the most accurate description that I can give, yet it doesn't satisfy the whole of what happens with a *Reiju*. It's a process or an "initiation" like nothing within our culture, and yet it works. We access something that I can only term as spiritual within each of us, master and student, even if the student isn't aware or doesn't think of themselves as spiritual. Through the *Reiju*, the master helps the student to become aware of, and therefore access, their own Reiki. We could describe it as a connection of essence: the master's essence connects with the student's essence. It's another part of the Reiki system that has to be experienced to be fully understood.

Our Reiki, the subtle energy within us, and the great Reiki of the universe are no different. They are one and the same; there is no separation. People get confused or misunderstand the nature of Reiki, because we often say it is "universal energy", and therefore we think that it's coming in from outside of us. We think "universal" means "universe" and therefore "out there". This is both true and untrue at the same time. Reiki is "out there", but it's also "in here", in every living thing.

When we connect with Reiki, we connect with all Reiki – within ourselves and out there … This becomes "one great Reiki"! When we are working on our self, we are not "bringing in" universal energy from outside. We are balancing and aligning our own physical, mental, emotional and spiritual self into a whole. We are connecting to our own universal energy, our own Reiki. Yet while doing this, we can often feel a deeper connection of oneness, which doesn't differentiate or feel separation; the oneness of self with all that is –the "great Reiki".

I think of this in terms of air. Air is all around us, all of the time, not just up there in the sky – it's why we can breathe. Yet we don't consciously think of air. We can't see it, smell it or touch it. When I breathe, I breathe in the air around me. When that air goes into my body, is it different to the air outside? When I breathe out, is that air different to the air still inside my body? In that breath, the air within me and outside of me become one. The energy of Reiki is exactly the same as this. All "one great Reiki"!

When the master performs the *Reiju*, it's a spiritual blessing that helps us to connect with what is already, and has always been, inside of us and all around us. The attunement, or *Reiju*, is like opening a door within us. The master shows us or guides us towards the metaphorical door that has always been there, but the master can't step through it for us – only we can do that.

The *Reiju* is integral to the system of Reiki, handed down from Mikao Usui. People ask if they can attune themselves to Reiki. The answer is that if you haven't had a *Reiju* from a Reiki master, the energy work you are practising isn't Reiki. That isn't to say that people can't work with energy or do energy healing without the Reiki *Reiju*. Many people are natural healers, but it isn't *Reiki* without the *Reiju*.

The *Reiju* offers something much deeper than a simple physical performance. It truly is a spiritual blessing, and every participant will have a different experience. For some it's immediate and profound, an obvious shift on some level that seems to open something inside of us. I have seen people with beatific smiles on their faces or in joyful tears. For others, the effect feels subtle and really not all that special. But just like everything with Reiki, it can be the effect that comes *afterwards*, what the *Reiju* can do for us in the longer term. It's also a safety net, guiding us in a safe way to work with energy and to access our own Reiki, our own *ki*, our own deeper self.

People who awaken to healing energy with no guide, mentor or spiritual framework may find themselves easily drained, tired, sick and not understanding boundaries or indeed what is happening when they heal others. Unless they already have an experienced mentor guiding them, whether Reiki based or not, figuring out energy healing alone can be difficult and challenging.

The Nature Of Reiki And Nature Reiki

Many students are already aware of the subtle underlying energy and have an ability, to a greater or lesser extent, to heal before they take their level one class. They are drawn to Reiki because they want to learn more, and this pathway seems to offer an attractive framework for healing to many people. Students who are already aware of their own energy and their ability to heal love the *Reiju* and the system of Reiki. Unlike some other energy-healing modalities, we are not using our own *ki*, our own energy, to heal others. We are accessing the universal *ki* to allow the recipient's body to heal itself.

Going back to our earlier analogy of Reiki being a field, perhaps we can say that we consciously, with intention, direct the field of energy for healing to occur. This is why Reiki tends to lift us up and help the healers to feel great afterwards, rather than drained, tired or sick, because of our connection with the great *ki*, the oneness. The practices within the system give a sense of gentleness and safety, as well as a structure to the work. In short, Reiki is comforting!

I like to think of Reiki in the following way. Imagine a kernel of energy within you, in your core. It is part of you, and has always been there. It may sprout by itself, creating a tiny shoot. When you have the level one *Reiju*, the seed opens, sprouting, or it grows a little more, becoming stronger. With your own hands-on self-Reiki, that seedling grows even more. Every practice you do, every hands-on session, every focus on the precepts, every meditation, helps to strengthen that seedling, so that it continues to grow into a strong, rooted big plant. Each successive *Reiju* helps that plant to grow even bigger and stronger. Your own continuing practice maintains and nurtures that plant within.

We all have Reiki, and we are all connected to the great Reiki. The *system* of Reiki, including the *Reiju*, helps us to understand and connect with our self and the great oneness of all in a safe, structured and nurturing way.

Nature Reiki

As all living things have Reiki, all of nature is filled with its own Reiki essence: every plant, shrub, flower and tree. Nature has its own Reiki, and it also responds incredibly well to receiving Reiki from us. Or perhaps it is better to say that it is very easy to connect with nature Reiki!

When we work with people, we have barriers to get through – both our own, and the recipient's. We have to get past all of our thoughts, doubts, fears and distractions. We are thinking about the hand positions, whether our touch is too firm or too light, what the client is thinking, and so on. We may find that our mind starts wandering, thinking about lunch, or our family, or things we have to do later. This is a natural state of the mind and happens to everyone. When we notice this, we gently bring our focus back to the *now*, to our client and Reiki. Often, we have to get through these barriers to the focus of oneness with Reiki.

This isn't so much the case with children, and it's easier the younger they are, right down to babies. This is because our small people haven't yet picked up all the barriers that we put in place with Reiki and energy. They simply accept what they experience, so Reiki flows instantly. You will have experienced this if you have ever given Reiki to a baby or young person. There's no waiting for that connection; it just happens. Often, we only need to give Reiki to our young for a short period of time. Because it flows without barriers, it doesn't need 30 minutes or an hour, even five minutes can be enough.

We find the same with animals and Reiki. As with children, the energy just flows, and animals of all and every kind will take from this exactly what they need. Each type of animal responds slightly differently to Reiki. I will talk about this in more detail a little further on.

If Reiki flows more easily through the young and through animals, imagine then the feel of Reiki with nature! We already know the effect that nature has on the human mind and body. Most of us have felt this; we only need to take a walk in the countryside, in the woods, by a river or mountains to experience the slowing down and calming of the mind, body and spirit. Being in nature has a positive and calming effect on us, whether we are spiritual or not!

When we are alert to our surroundings and walk consciously in nature, we become even more aware of this gentling effect. The Japanese even have a term for this: "forest bathing" – *Shinrin Yoku*. I wholeheartedly believe that nature is the best medicine for anger, sadness, melancholy and troubles of the spirit. If you don't believe me, try it. Go and take a walk. Spend some time in nature. Don't rush. Sit and while away some time. Look at the views. Meander back home slowly … and check in on yourself and see how you feel after your walk.

What happens if we connect with Reiki in nature? We can try this in different ways, such as with a house plant, in our garden, with a tree, at your favourite place to visit in nature, or with a patch of grass in a park or an open field.

With a house plant, sit or stand with your hands on or around the plant, or with your palms on the soil. Focus on Reiki and the plant. See what happens and notice how you feel. For me, the feeling is one of calm and gentility. When we do this, we give Reiki to the plant … but we also *receive* Reiki. Or perhaps we are just open to the one great Reiki that is accessible through connection with the plant.

If we just want to connect with Reiki when we are outside, rather than having a specific focus, then just sit as if in meditation, on the lawn or on the ground in the woods. Place your hands however they feel comfortable – palms face up in your lap, in *Gassho* (prayer position), or at the root, sacral or heart chakra position. Allow yourself to connect with Reiki and focus on just *being* where you are, aware of your surroundings. Allow yourself to just experience. To just *be*. For me, it feels like an instant connection with the one great Reiki. It feels immediate, open and incredibly peaceful. Take your time and spend as long as you like in the experience.

Reiki in a garden is lovely. Whether you sit on the lawn or focus on a patch of plants, vegetable plot or tree, the result is the same. When you want to focus on something specific, place your hands where it feels natural to do so: either on the soil or directly touching your subject – perfect when connecting with trees, hands on the bark – or near to but not touching the subject, which is good for delicate plants or growing vegetables.

Again, connect with Reiki and focus on your tree, plant or vegetables. Allow yourself to experience, to feel. Be open; don't try – just *be*. What do you feel? For me, it's an instant reciprocity; an instant opening up, a *being-ness*. We may be giving out Reiki, but we are also connected with all Reiki: we feel the energy of the plants, the tree and of nature. We become one with it. Reiki in nature of any kind is a truly beautiful feeling, and it really is like medicine for the spirit.

You may ask if nature has its own Reiki, why then do we need to give Reiki to a tree, plant or growing vegetables? I think this is because we can all do with a boost, and in giving Reiki we are giving nature a little extra – a helping hand. We help her to be well, to grow more healthy and to strengthen. I also see it as an act of love because we are sharing ourselves, and sharing being part of the great connection. We are simply stepping into the connection, participating. Giving Reiki to nature is the equivalent of hugging another person. It's an act that says, "I care, and I want to connect." In turn, nature shares its Reiki, its essence, its *being-ness* with us … and we feel that totality, that openness that *is*.

Animal Reiki

Many books and courses deal specifically with Reiki for animals. If you would like to work professionally with animal Reiki, it may be worth looking into these, particularly if you want to work in association with vets, animal charity organisations, and so on, for them to take Reiki seriously. They may require you to have an in-depth knowledge of animal anatomy and physiology.

On an informal level, however, of course we can give Reiki to animals, just as we do to each other. We can give Reiki to any type of creature, from an insect to a bird, and to pets of all sizes, including horses. I even give Reiki to our family goldfish! I simply place my hands on the glass and allow energy to flow. Our goldfish swims around in the area where my hands are.

In very general terms, for animal Reiki, trust your instincts: place your hands where it feels comfortable and natural to do so, and of course where it's comfortable for the animal. There is no point trying to place your hands somewhere you think is right but causes discomfort to the animal. If it's a small creature, such as a pet hamster or gerbil, and they are fine with being handled, simply pick them up as usual and just allow Reiki to flow. Such a creature is small enough that Reiki will naturally go everywhere without the need for chakra placements or specific areas.

Do this for as long as it's comfortable for your pet, which may be just a few minutes. A bigger creature such as a rabbit may require a few hand placements to reach everywhere, or you can hold your hands in one position on either side of the rabbit, for as long as the rabbit is comfortable with this. You will know when they have had enough as they will want to move away. Let them do so, as you don't want to cause them any stress.

Each individual will be more or less receptive to Reiki: some rabbits may happily stay in your lap, or if they are on the floor they will stay in one position with your hands on them for quite some time. Others may want to move away after a minute or two, having had quite enough of that, thank you! Always be mindful of your pet's comfort.

Cats appear to be highly receptive to Reiki, but often only need very little. They seem to know exactly how much they need, to the extent that they will take a little from you, sitting with your hands placed along their back or sides, or wherever is comfortable for you and your cat, and then leap out of the way the very moment they have had enough. Sometimes they are happy to sit and soak it up for a while, purring contentedly next to you or on your lap, particularly if they are unwell or depleted. If they are perfectly balanced in their own energy though, they won't tolerate a lick of Reiki! They will simply stalk off, and perhaps look back at you as if to say, "What do you think you are doing?" Always be guided by your cat!

Dogs on the other hand seem much more accepting and tolerant of flowing energy, soaking up as much as they can take. They will often sit quite happily, with your hands in any natural position – along their back, sides or chest – absorbing that warm feeling. I have heard many stories of dogs shuffling and moving around so that the human's hands are in the exact place that they, the dog, require them to be. Afterwards when they have had enough, they simply lay calmly, often falling asleep. Again, I have heard many stories of "highly active" dogs becoming calm and quiet after Reiki. If they do move out of the way, allow them to do so, as they are telling you that they have had enough.

Animal Reiki is a lovely feeling, because the animals simply accept, and we do it for them without expecting anything in return ... the act itself is enough. Just like with nature, giving Reiki to pets and animals of all kinds is a gesture that says, "I care, I connect with you." It is an act of love.

Always be guided by your animal. Don't force them or hold them tightly, as this will only cause them stress. Make sure that your hand placements are comfortable for them, not pressing hard on their temples or high on their throat, for example. Most importantly, there is absolutely no replacement for a vet's check-up and advice. If a pet is poorly, a vet's visit is vital. Reiki is a wonderful *complementary* therapy, but it can't replace a professional medical examination.

Go out there and have fun with Reiki! Try nature Reiki and animal Reiki. Allow yourself to be open to whatever the experience brings.

Summary

- Everything living has "Reiki", its own essence – humans, animals and nature.
- The *Reiju* from the master doesn't give us Reiki, but helps us to connect and become aware of our own innate Reiki.
- Our own inner Reiki and the "universal energy" are really one and the same – this is no-separation, oneness.
- The system of Reiki, which includes the *Reiju*, creates a structured, nurturing way in which to practise energy healing.
- Nature has its own Reiki, and we can connect with this when we sit with focus in nature.
- Trust your instincts and let the experience guide you – just be open.
- Animals of every size and type can be given Reiki.
- Have fun with nature Reiki and animal Reiki … It is a truly marvellous experience!

15. Depression, Anxiety And Reiki

"Remember... the entrance door to the sanctuary is inside you."

- Rumi

Depression and anxiety are common in society and often (but not always) go hand in hand. Depression affects us on every level of our being, and anxiety can be debilitating, affecting the choices we make in life – for example, choosing not to go out with friends or to engage in certain social activities because it would cause an anxiety or panic attack. I have seen many clients with depression and anxiety, either as singular or combined conditions. Reiki has had a positive effect in most cases, bringing some calm and lifting the severity of the issue, at least for a time.

It used to be the case that people would say, "Depression? You just need to cheer up!" Or "Go for a walk and get over yourself!" Now thankfully most people are aware that depression is a lot more complex and serious than this. It affects the mind so much that people may feel that there is no joy or hope in life. Low levels of the "happy hormones", serotonin and dopamine, are linked to depression. Sufferers may have more aches and pains, as well as susceptibility to illnesses due to a potentially lowered immune system. The lack of dopamine means that depression can lead to more tiredness, which is why some sufferers may sleep more than normal. Mentally, it feels as though a fog has descended on the mind, cutting off any sense of joy or love. It's not that people don't want to cheer up; they literally can't.

If we look at depression in relation to the chakras, we can see that depression can affect every single one, removing us from every part of our inner self. Every single energy centre is depleted and off balance. We may:

- become cut off from our sense of connection and spirituality (crown)
- become closed to our inner awareness and intuition (third eye)
- find it difficult to express our emotional needs or to communicate effectively (throat)
- have very little or no sense of self-love and find it difficult to maintain relationships (heart)
- suffer from a lack of motivation, self-esteem and self-worth (solar plexus)
- become unable to process emotions and more likely to indulge in our own personal addictions, whether food, cigarettes, drink or drugs (sacral)
- find our sense of safety and security is also probably at a low ebb (root)

Anxiety feels both mental and physical. It creates thoughts in the mind – "I can't deal with this," or "This is scary," or "Something is going to go wrong" – and also hits the person with a physical feeling too: the heart speeds up and feels like it's racing, the stomach gets a wave of butterflies. All of this combined triggers an anxiety or a panic attack. A panic attack isn't harmful, but it feels like it at the time. Some people feel like they are going to die, the effect is that severe.

Anxiety can, like depression, be nebulous in its origins, appearing seemingly from nowhere, although it often stems from a particular source (or trigger), even if we can't recognise it. The reasons, triggers and symptoms of anxiety vary for each person, but I do think that in some cases at least, there is an underlying issue of feeling out of control – whether that is fear of the future, or because of something that has happened in the past. Feeling that life is beyond our control or that we lack control in our own life can lead to this feeling of anxiety.

An anxiety or panic attack, however, can be triggered at seemingly innocuous times. The link between our direct thoughts and when an attack happens appears very tenuous. When we are already in "anxiety mode", our brains and bodies are in the flight or fight response and are already poised to deal with a threat. When something happens that we don't like, even something small – such as standing in a big crowd of people we don't know, having to enter a place we don't want to be in, or a critical comment – that is enough to tip us over the edge and for our brain to interpret this as a predator threat. It literally sets off an alarm bell in our head, and the only way our system knows how to deal with this is – panic.

We often find that anxiety, in relation to the chakras, affects the crown and third eye, heart, solar plexus and sacral. It may affect all of them or some of them – it's different for each individual, but these are the main areas where we may find a strong imbalance. By completing a full Reiki treatment on someone with anxiety, we bring calm and balance to every chakra point, to the mind and to the body, and switch them back to the relaxation response, which is particularly important and effective in this case.

When someone regains a sense of inner calm and balance, an issue that may usually trigger anxiety is seen objectively and doesn't become a major stumbling point. The more a person is able to do this, the more they are regaining control from the anxiety reaction. Their brain is learning new pathways and not to react in that habitual "fight or flight" response. This is also why mindfulness-based meditations and activities are good for anxiety, because these teach people how to focus on the very present moment. This then pulls the brain's attention to what is happening *now* rather than what it fears has happened or may yet happen.

Depression is deep and complex. In my own personal experience, Reiki has the greatest effect when we start to get to the *root cause* of the issue. We may well be able to help mitigate the severity of the effects of depression, as well as anxiety, through Reiki treatments, but we need to remember that Reiki isn't a miracle cure, and we can't say that we will "cure" either condition. Reiki may help someone who is suffering, but to what extent and in what time-frame is going to be on a case-by-case basis.

Reiki may be able to help a person deal with some of the symptoms and the effects of depression, keeping them on a more even keel than they would be without Reiki. It may give someone a boost, helping them to see a little way through the mental or emotional fog that depression brings, perhaps helping them to clarify or understand their condition – or even simply to accept the "bad days" and be able to surrender those days and write them off: just getting through that day (or those days) until a good day arrives. The thing with depression is that someone doesn't feel low and depressed every single day: you can feel okay one day or for a few days, and then the next week have a few days of feeling like everything is hopeless. It can come in waves. Understanding this and being able to put coping mechanisms into place can be really helpful in getting through those low periods.

Reiki can help to minimise some of the ongoing symptoms and to boost the immune system, but it may take a while. Getting to the root cause of depression isn't easy, and quite often people don't know what the root cause is. They may not even realise that they have depression for a number of weeks or even months, until they perceive that life isn't what they used to think it was, or a doctor gives them a diagnosis. Depression can often be subtle and insidious. It doesn't just happen, but understanding how or why we feel depressed can be challenging. There is some evidence to suggest that some people have a genetic propensity towards depression, particularly if there is a family history. This isn't the only reason though, and other possible causes may include:

- an ongoing unhealthy situation, whether due to a relationship, family, unsupportive friend circle, work or other issue.
- unhealthy beliefs or misconceptions about your personal life or the world around you (unable to see the truth of matters and instead believing things that aren't actually true), or poor coping mechanisms that can include addictions or behaviours we know aren't good for us but that we continue to do because they are born of old habits.
- "crap life syndrome", which is a new concept that is currently being put forward – i.e. being in a financial situation that makes life very hard and causes constant high-level stress; having poor work conditions and feeling undervalued or unappreciated; being in a housing situation that isn't right for us and are unable to move to a better situation.
- possible chemical imbalance in the brain, causing a physical association for depression to occur.

The root cause is, of course, going to be different for each person. Barring physiological reasons, I do think there is a main commonality for the occurrence of depression, and that is a lack of purpose. Or having a clear purpose but lacking the means to achieve it. I think that feeling we have a sense of purpose in life is the foundation of our happiness and lust for life. Having a sense of purpose is what not only gets us out of bed in the mornings but aids us in *looking forward* to the day. For some people, that sense of purpose comes with their job – some people are lucky enough to have found what they love doing and live it every day. For others, it may not be the day job, but the ambition to create music, art or writing. For others, it may be serving their community.

What it is *not* is "being rich" just for the sake of having money. This doesn't equate to purpose. People who are "rich", who have more than enough money, can suffer from sadness and depression too, because money doesn't create a sense of personal purpose in life. However, a lack of enough money to pay the bills and do what needs to be done can of course cause stress, which can lead to depression. It isn't easy to be able to get out of such a difficult financial situation. We can't always immediately change our current circumstances, but we may be able to find ways to make it easier, or to have longer term goals that can help us. If we can focus on what we can do to improve our situation, and work towards that, then that may give us a sense of purpose.

Our sense of purpose may not be what we think it is: some people are surprised to find that when they start doing some charity work or volunteering, or helping out in their community in some way, this gives them such a mental and emotional lift that it actually *becomes* their purpose. For others, it may be a chance to try something that they never thought they would have the chance to do, or that they would even like! Indeed, in his book *Happiness, A guide to developing life's most important skill*, Matthieu Ricard states that:

"Happiness rises with social involvement and participation in volunteer organisations, the practice of sports or music ... It is closely tied to the maintenance and quality of private relationships."

Finding our purpose isn't always easy. It does take work and some internal analysing, examination and patience. There has been some research done into the idea of happiness, and whether it can be cultivated rather than just experienced. There are certain things that we can do to help ourselves develop both purpose and happiness. In a later section of his book, Ricard discusses a study undertaken by M Seligman, the pioneer of positive psychology, who asked his students to firstly do an activity of enjoyment and then to perform a random act of kindness. He says this about the study:

"The satisfaction triggered by a pleasant activity, such as going out with friends ... were largely eclipsed by those deriving from performing an act of kindness. When the act was spontaneous and drew on humane qualities, the entire day was improved; the subjects noticed that they were better listeners that day, more friendly, and more appreciated by others."

Therefore, it appears that empathic and kind acts engender greater feeling in our own self of self-worth, belief and happiness.

When we have a Reiki treatment, this brings calm and balance to our inner self, but it may also help us to achieve a sense of clarity, and through this we may begin to discover the origins of our anxiety or depression. We could even, through Reiki, find our purpose, or what it is that we need to move forwards.

Mind and control

Some years ago, I went through a period of depression and anxiety. Depression came first, and anxiety grew from that condition. There were times when I thought I was going crazy: my mind, my thoughts, felt too big to control, too big to make sense. I felt like I couldn't trust my own mind. The thoughts in there were chaotic, and not mine. They were coming into me from outside, and I couldn't make sense of them. This is what happens when we don't pay attention to our mind – so many of our thoughts are not thoughts that we think, but things that just happen to wander through. Most of the time, we can either ignore them or entertain them.

Most often, we are not actually consciously *thinking*; we are allowing our mind to roam free, doing whatever it likes, and we simply accept the thoughts that we have. But what happens when those thoughts go wrong? When you suddenly find that you don't agree with your own thoughts, or they don't make sense to you. Or you have conflicting thoughts in your head at the same time. In this case, we become very aware that our own mind is actually a separate entity from *Me*, the thing we call *I*. And this is, I can tell you, a very disturbing awareness to have, when we are not in control. I can't escape my own mind – so what do I do with these thoughts that I don't agree with or can't understand?

Once I understood that I couldn't trust my own mind, I let the thoughts rampage, just watching them like an observer, like a visitor to the cinema, until they simply blew away like passing clouds. I stopped trying to think or do anything, and just let those thoughts run their course, knowing that they were absolutely nothing to do with me. I stepped back from my own mind, recognising the thoughts as separate to myself and choosing not to attach any significance to them.

The other thing that helped me with both my mind and the feelings of anxiety in my body was conscious breathing and energy work. For breathing, I would breathe nice and deeply, to and from the *hara*, just focusing on taking that breath down into my body, way down past my navel. By doing this, all of my awareness – mind, body and emotions – became focused on one thing: my breath, into my body. I was taking my attention *away* from the feelings of anxiety and giving that attention to my very real self – my body. That brought my awareness to *within* me, and away from external distractions and illusions of fear and being out of control. It brought me to a place of centredness, and therefore control. Once we become present *within our self*, we are able to take control, remain calm and *just be*.

The energy work that I did was a particular visual meditation, which is given at the end of this chapter. The point of all this is that we *come back to our self, whole, fully aware*. In this way, being aware and present of our whole self and current circumstances and surroundings, we are clear in our mind and body. Therefore any issues, obstacles or problems that are thrown our way come to us at our centre, where we are able to absorb them, *accept them for what they are* and then deal with them.

Dealing with depression and anxiety isn't easy, and it can take time to move through these conditions, but we may be able to help ourselves in some ways and at least mitigate the worst of the effects. I found, as many other sufferers of anxiety and depression have, that gardening was immensely helpful. Gardening is mindful; it felt meditative to me. When you start gardening, it pulls you in. Your whole focus is on what you are doing, and the mind stops its distracting, chaotic thoughts, instead just focusing on the soil, on planting, weeding or whatever it is you are currently doing.

Finding an activity such as gardening, or something else that has that same effect, can be one extra way of helping ourselves by:

- paying attention inwards, to our mind and body
- focusing on our breath and energy
- understanding how the mind works, and what is coming in the mind which we don't have direct control over
- finding, if we can, the source of the condition – what started it, where it came from – although this isn't always easy or indeed even possible
- maybe finding a purpose that we can focus on and engage with, that absorbs us and even brings us some happiness

Reiki can help us through giving us enough space to be able to mentally breathe; to lift the stress of these conditions enough to find ways to help ourselves, and also working wonderfully alongside the other helpful activities, such as gardening. Reiki may well be the first step on the path back to wellness, to finding the answers to be able to either move through our mental condition, or to heal into wholeness.

Summary

- Depression and anxiety are common today and are conditions that feel as though they are held in both the mind and the body.
- Reiki can often help to calm and balance the severity of each condition.
- There are a variety of reasons why someone may suffer from anxiety and depression, and we can look to see if we can get to the root cause, as well as treating the symptoms.
- Finding a purpose, whether through work, charity or volunteer work, social engagements or an activity that absorbs us, can help us to move through anxiety and depression.
- We may be able to help ourselves when we understand how the mind works, by concentrating on our mind and our body and engaging with meditation practices.

Exercise: energy visualisation for re-centering

- Sit comfortably as if in meditation.
- Take a slow, gentle deep breath, down to your *hara*, below your navel.
- Imagine, sense or feel earth energy coming up from the ground (you can visualise this as a colour if you like; any colour is fine).
- Allow this earth energy to come up through your feet, up to your *hara*. Pause, feeling it flow here, then continue all the way up to your crown, at the top of your head.
- Gently release all the way back down.
- Breathe to your *hara*.
- Imagine, sense or feel heavenly energy (again, you can visualise this as a colour, whichever colour feels right to you) coming down from above, entering your crown, slowly down to your heart and then navel, pausing here, then continuing all the way down to your feet.
- Gently release.
- Again, bring earth energy up in the same way as before; release and repeat with heavenly energy coming down from above through your crown and all the way down.
- Repeat for as long as you wish.
- On the final release, sit for a few minutes, breathing to your *hara*, being aware of yourself, your inner body and how you feel. Take these moments to just experience yourself.
- Nice and gently, bring yourself back.

16. Can I Use Reiki For: Weight Issues; Eating Disorders; Stopping Smoking; Drug Or Alcohol Recovery?

> "The first peace, which is the most important, is that which comes within the souls of people when they realise their relationship, their oneness, with the universe and all its powers, and when they realise that at the centre of the universe dwells Wakan-Tanka, and that this centre is really everywhere, it is within each of us."
>
> - *Black Elk*

Addictions of any kind, whether to food, tobacco, alcohol or drugs, can be symptomatic of an emotional root cause as a maladaptive method of trying to deal with something painful that has happened, or is happening, in our lives. Addiction occurs when the coping mechanism we put in place to deal with difficulties gets beyond our control and becomes a habit, causing a physical or psychological reliance.

Put simply – Reiki can help with a particular issue and help us to recover or resolve a problem or habit that no longer serves our highest good. However, it's worth remembering that Reiki can only help when we really want it to, and when we do the work alongside it – that is, to take the holistic approach and look at all of the factors involved in each case, and to take the appropriate steps to help ourselves along the way. It ought to go without saying that other appropriate help should be sought where necessary.

Reiki helps to align us with our inner being, our "true self", to bring positive and lasting changes. Substantive results are going to take some time – unless one of those Reiki miracles occurs. We still need to put the work in to give ourselves the greatest chance of achieving our new improved state. Ongoing sessions over a period of time, and alongside any other appropriate intervention such as medicines or therapy, can be a great boost and benefit in achieving the desired result.

There are three main ways that Reiki may help us to give up the habits that we want to change, our problems and addictions:

- Identify and begin to deal with the root cause of the problem, if there is a root cause (why and when did the problem start?).
- Turn down the volume on the craving or driving force of the habit.
- Help to improve coping mechanisms and the ability to manage emotional ups and downs – in other words, improving our emotional self-reliance.

There can be a perception of Reiki healing as being all sparkly, light and good. Quite often it is, leaving us with a floaty feeling and a natural high after a session. We would do well to remember that healing isn't always light and fluffy: think about when we fall down and hurt ourselves. Bruising, scrapes and even breaks and fractures … as these heal, they can cause uncomfortable and painful sensations as our body knits itself back together.

Alcohol and drug recovery is healing. It's healing from our habit of addiction that, if allowed to continue for a long period, becomes not only our emotional crutch and ability to cope when we feel that things are going badly, but also causes physical degradation as well. Addiction to certain drugs become physical, causing the body itself to continually crave the drug. Long-term alcohol addiction can potentially cause problems with the liver and the healthy functioning of most organs. Unhealthy relationships with food can lead to anorexia or bulimia, while on the other end of the spectrum, weight gain can put stress on our body and our internal organs. Moving through addiction of any kind is hard – really hard – but is itself a healing process.

Identifying the root cause

When we use Reiki as a vehicle for healing and change, that healing can also throw up some challenges, such as unpacking deep-seated emotional issues or trauma. These need to be addressed and dealt with if they come up, in an appropriate manner, to facilitate healing and recovery of addiction or unhealthy relationships (with food or, indeed, people).

As an illustrative example of how Reiki may help us in these instances, firstly, it can help to declutter and destress the mind, bringing a sense of calm and well-being. Once a person feels relaxed and better in themselves, Reiki may uncover questions of where our habits came from. What is the blockage to recovery? Where did it start from? Why did it start? Are there emotional issues to be released?

There may be old trauma, and any type of addiction or unhealthy relationships could be a response to dealing with that trauma. If we can look at the beginning of the cycle of our habit, we may begin to move through this and heal, as we are able to see that the coping mechanism is no longer needed. This may take the form of seeking counselling, cognitive behavioural therapy (CBT) or other therapy, or it may be enough to acknowledge it and understand where our current journey began. Reiki healing may feel uncomfortable for some people as they perceive the difficult circumstances that they had to deal with, but understanding that they are no longer in that place can be a helpful motivation in releasing old patterns.

Every individual has their own story, and some may not want to consciously unpack old emotional issues, finding it too difficult to revisit. Reiki works *for and with* the individual, so the healing release may occur without having to discuss or open up old emotional issues, but the thought processes or emotional healing may still take place on a more subtle, rather than direct, level. Any such release can be uncomfortable for some people, but we should remember that it's still a healing process and a necessary step that we may need to go through. Or it may not happen in this way – it may happen gradually, subtly, simply allowing the person to begin to feel better in themselves, gently releasing the old, stored emotions or thought patterns that feed the ongoing habit.

Turning down the volume

Reiki has been known to help lessen the craving itself, so it has an effect on the physical as well as the psychological responses. This instant relief of craving, needless to say, goes a long way to helping someone move to a new way of being and moving out the other side of addiction. Again, this happens on an individual basis *so it can never be guaranteed as an outcome, but it may be achieved over time.*

For people who have an eating disorder and are underweight because of an imbalance in their relationship with food, the craving isn't with food but is often in the desire to maintain some control in their lives. The reason behind the disorder is what Reiki will focus on here – what is driving the response. When we can get to this, hopefully Reiki will help to turn down the need for that particular response.

For those who struggle with weight gain, eating too much may be a symptom of something else: eating to stop thinking; to stop feeling guilty; to cover the emotions that are the *cause* of overeating. Again, Reiki gets to where it needs to go – the desire or the craving *behind* the actions. Once the volume is turned down on this, maintaining control and willpower becomes much easier. We come into a state of balance in ourselves, and find that our eating habits aren't difficult to change but rather evolve naturally.

Throughout this, we or our client still need to have the focus, the true desire, to want to change – to lose weight, stop smoking or be alcohol or drug free. Reiki helps us in the best way when we engage with it with intention, so we may still need to put the necessary work in as well. This may involve following a programme to help with alcohol recovery, for example, or following a dietary nutrition plan, or the first step may even be admitting, "I'm not coping and I need help."

By the fourth, fifth, or sixth session, the temptation to lapse may be a peripheral feeling more than one difficult to resist. It may even happen after the first session; once again, the journey is going to be as individual as each person, so we can't make any guarantees about when or how much Reiki will help. We all need to be guided by our own experience in that current time.

Emotional self-reliance

Reiki can help our determination. It can help our mind change track, focusing on our will to heal ourselves. It can help us deal with the emotions that come up through such changes, and it can enable us to change our perception of our habits and their origins. Reiki facilitates our healing from the inside out, gradually aligning us with who we really are inside, cleansing and releasing any imbalances and disturbances within, which in turn helps us to change the course of who we are on the outside. Therefore, by cleansing and clearing old emotions, problem areas or negative thought patterns, we change how we perceive ourselves, and what we feel we can and can't do.

We may find that we have a stronger self-belief. The act of a Reiki session may also enhance our own willpower and motivation, so instead of a downward spiral we create an upward spiral: having the determination to deal with our issues and wanting to change – having a Reiki treatment – coming out with a stronger motivation and willpower – more determined to achieve our goal, and so on.

When we have a sense of inner strength, any emotional turbulence that comes into our life, or any of our own thoughts that used to create fear, guilt, anger or shame, become something we realise that we can deal with. Again we may find that we can move through it without being thrown off balance. When we do this once, a source of pride wells up from within. This positive feeling is such a psychological reward that we know we can do it again – and again and again. We have reached a place of self-reliance.

The other way Reiki may help us to achieve this is by helping our minds to relax and enter a state of calm. In this calm space, we can perceive our own thoughts in a different way, flipping them into their opposite. If we have a negative thought, what happens if we flip this? What if the opposite of what we are thinking is instead true? Suddenly the story that we tell ourselves is no longer the only version, nor the true one. When we see this new way of thinking, we understand that *we can control our thoughts rather than merely accepting thoughts that we have*. This realisation is incredibly empowering.

In all cases, Reiki can help us to gain a sense of self love, filling the gap that we may be trying to fill with food, alcohol, drugs or control mechanisms. Reiki can aid recovery and change of any unhelpful habits in essentially the same way.

- Focus on the specific issue to be helped.
- Have regular ongoing sessions of Reiki, as often as possible or as required.
- Discuss the mental state of the person, and their determination and desire to effect change – or think about this consciously, if doing this for yourself.
- Visualise life as you want it to be – free of the addiction. Visualisation can help to improve focus, motivation and the

manifestation of the desired outcome.

- Discuss anything that comes up through the Reiki treatments, including potentially emotional areas that may be the cause, or a part of the cause, for the addiction or relationship with food. If doing this for yourself, write this down in a journal or discuss the issues with a trusted friend or partner or another Reiki healer.
- Allow healing to occur from the inside out, focusing on what seems to need healing at that particular session, i.e. dealing with the emotional issues, sense of vulnerability or the determination to stay on track.
- Understand the link between the body, mind and spirit, and that each of these plays a part in our habits and decisions.
- Offer a space of support, non-judgement and safety, if healing another, and for ourselves being mindful of having a non-judgemental attitude and not being self-critical (treating self as we would another person).
- Look at how Reiki can help alongside other support, and have a programme for the client to follow, such as changing triggers and having a new "go-to" when temptation arises (what can we do instead of going to our habitual response? – speak to someone, go running, punch a pillow, hug a tree); counselling; other complementary therapies such as acupuncture or appropriate medical treatments.
- For ourselves, it's especially important to notice the sensations and after-effects of Reiki, where the healing feels it is re-balancing and aligning (which areas feel strongest?), to gain a deeper understanding.

Paying attention to any strong emotions that arise, or that make us feel uncomfortable during a Reiki session – such as sudden anger, irritability, deep sadness or anxiety – will give us an indication of what we are dealing with, what stage we are at with our recovery, and where deep-rooted problems may lie. Dealing with these emotional responses isn't peripheral but is central to the issue at hand, as they can be playing a part in our continuing habits. Once we address the underlying issues and help to release or change these, recovery and a new way of doing things can become much easier.

It's worth saying that if we, as a person trained in Reiki, find ourselves wanting to change an old habit such as an addiction or our relationship with food, we may be able to do this ourselves with Reiki. However, we may also find it useful and beneficial to get help from another Reiki practitioner. Having an outside helper can be of use if we have emotional issues to move through, as they will be able to focus on us without the internal dialogue, habits and lifetime of assumptions that we have built up in our inner world. I do think that having another Reiki practitioner alongside us is of particular benefit the more serious the issue is. We can continue to help ourselves with Reiki, but extra help can never be a bad thing.

Reiki can kick start our desire to change and help us to maintain that desire and our will. It can make determined changes easier and help us with any emotional issues that may arise because of these changes. When we feel more positive in our mind state, when we feel more positive about ourselves, we are far more likely to want to and be able to effect positive changes in our lives, and this sense of positivity, calm and well-being is exactly what Reiki gives us.

The issue of weight gain may be to do with enjoying too much food that is bad for us (easy to do with a western diet, with all of the salt, sugars and fats that are put into our foods). Carbohydrates, for example, found in bread, pasta and potatoes, affect the hormonal balance of insulin, which changes the way that our cells process energy, and causes our body to store fat. Carbohydrates are also addictive, so it can be easy to eat more of them than is actually healthy. However, weight gain may be caused by biochemical or genetic factors, or it may be down to emotional issues and habits – such as low self-esteem, childhood issues or relationship breakdowns. There are many reasons why some of us are perhaps not the weight that we would like to be, or that we have an unhealthy relationship with food.

It may be that through the course of Reiki healing and the effect this engenders in our mind and spirit, we decide that actually our weight isn't the problem we thought it was. We may realise that in actual fact we are perfectly happy with who we are as a person. This is integral to Reiki as a holistic treatment – to show us who we truly are and to bring about a sense of self-compassion and self-love. We may come to realise that the problem, in fact, is literally the weight of other peoples' expectations of us; that actually we are comfortable and happy with who we are, how we are, in which case we don't need to worry!

If we are happy with ourselves, other peoples' opinions have no bearing. People will always have their opinions of us, and we will never be able to please everyone. So how we feel about ourselves is the only thing that we need to focus on and be happy with. If we do want to lose weight to feel good in ourselves, Reiki deals with the holistic approach – not just losing weight, but all of the issues around the weight gain, and our appreciation for (or lack of) our self.

Even if you have a setback during the course of your desire and intention to change, try not to worry about it. We are all human beings, and none of us are perfect. Prochaska and DiClemente produced the *Transtheoretical model of the stages of change* (1977), to show how people function when it comes to changing behaviours and habits. The model shows the stages as follows:

- Precontemplation, 'not ready'
- Contemplation, 'getting ready'
- Preparation, 'ready'
- Action

- Maintenance
- Relapse
- Back to the beginning, precontemplation

This pattern was described as a spiral rather than a circle, to show that people underwent this cycle numerous times, so from "relapse" we may then go back to "precontemplation" when we are ready to try and break our addiction or change our behaviour again. This model illustrates that it isn't at all uncommon to have a setback, even when we are determined and willing to change.

We can see from this that setbacks may happen, and putting pressure on ourselves or another to change in a certain way and within a certain time-frame isn't going to be helpful. Keep going with Reiki! Notice the positive changes. Which benefits have you found from regular Reiki? What have you noticed that has changed? Give yourself, or your recipient, the pats on the back that you deserve for every change, every step forward, every release from old patterns, habits and desires. Positive reinforcement has a much stronger effect on us than criticism does.

Effecting a positive change for any habit may take weeks or even months. The time it takes depends upon the individual, their experience and underlying issues. It may even be something that a person needs for years, with ongoing regular Reiki sessions to maintain their sense of well-being.

The same focus of using the practice and healing of Reiki to help with a specific issue can be applied to anything. Some further examples of direct focus are:

- issues around self-confidence and improvement
- stage fright or intense shyness
- breaking any old habits or patterns that no longer serve us
- anger issues
- anxiety issues

Can I Use Reiki For: Weight Issues; Eating Disorders; Stopping Smoking; Drug Or Alcohol Recovery?

All we need to do in any case that affects us personally is to focus on our goal and breaking the old habits, and think about how we want to improve, bringing this into our Reiki work.

To talk or not to talk

The beautiful thing – well, *one of* the beautiful things – about Reiki is that it isn't a talking therapy. Some people get an awful lot out of talking therapies such as counselling, and these can be incredibly beneficial. But there are times when a person isn't ready to talk about their experiences, or they reach a point where they just don't want to talk anymore. This puts them off receiving treatments and they will refuse to go any further with any type of counselling, because they can't face the emotional turbulence or stress that it will bring it up.

Reiki is great for people in this instance because they don't have to talk about their issues. They can come to a Reiki session knowing that it is a relaxation therapy, and they can just experience the treatment in terms of sensations and the after-effects, such as peace, well-being and centredness. Of course we should have a chat with someone as to why they want a Reiki session, whether they have a specific issue that they want help with, and what their expectations are. The more information that we, as the healer, have, the more we know about that person and where and how to focus the session. But Reiki does what it does for and with that person, so we don't have to have extensive and detailed information. A person can come to us and say, "I want Reiki for physical pains" … "for emotional issues" … "for stress…" We don't have to push someone to give us more information than they are comfortable with. If someone comes to us and doesn't want to talk, we can allow them just to experience the healing energy of Reiki, helping them to relax, find some peace and calm, and feel better in body and mind.

Conversely, some people find it helpful to talk and will want to tell us a lot of information – literally "getting something off their chest". This in itself is therapy. Our job as a Reiki practitioner isn't to judge or give advice, but it's just to listen. To be there. Sometimes this is all someone needs. It's fine for us to offer suggestions and be empathetic, discussing the person's own experience in an appropriate manner. If a person needs to talk, this can make them feel better before even having the Reiki treatment, doing part of the job before we begin the session.

Whether or not a person decides to talk, we still pick up a lot of information from them. Their mannerisms, attitude, posture and amount of eye contact will all give us cues into how that person is feeling, and how to relate to them. Someone who seems very anxious and nervous, for example, isn't going to be put at ease if we are very bubbly, animated and loud! Our own actions, behaviour and speech should all be keyed in to helping the recipient feel as safe and relaxed as possible. Talking from the client is optional: Reiki will help that person for their own benefit.

Summary

- Reiki can help with issues such as weight loss, eating disorders, stopping smoking, and alcohol and drug recovery.
- We should manage expectations and never assume that Reiki will help – but that it may help.
- These issues have a variety of factors and can be complex, and we should always take the individual's experience into account.
- Reiki works to help bring balance and alignment to a person's mind, body and spirit.
- It's through helping a person feel better in themselves, from the inside out, that Reiki can help us keep to the right track for the desired goal.
- Reiki can work wonderfully alongside any other treatment,

Can I Use Reiki For: Weight Issues; Eating Disorders; Stopping Smoking; Drug Or Alcohol Recovery?

whether this is medical or complementary.
- Reiki helps to reduce stress and release old emotions, coming to a place of peace and calm, and helping to restore a healthy and relaxed mind state and therefore, body.
- Reiki can help with any specific habit that we wish to change and improvements of self that we wish to make.
- A client can choose to talk or not to in a Reiki session, whatever feels comfortable to them. We don't need to push them for information.

17. Infertility, Pregnancy And Babies

"We are born of love; love is our mother"

- *Rumi*

Issues of fertility, infertility and pregnancy are deeply personal and sensitive. This is another specific issue that people ask whether Reiki can help as a treatment.

No Reiki healer or practitioner should *ever* tell someone, "Yes! I can *definitely* help you to have a baby!" *We don't know*, and we can never know what the outcome for an individual may be. Let us also remember that Reiki isn't about what *we want*, but about healing that person in that space and time, with no judgements, expectations or attachments. What will happen will happen.

In my practice I have seen a few people who required help with this particular issue, and a pregnancy happened at some point after their Reiki sessions. However, I can't know for certain whether that was solely down to the effect of Reiki, other medical or complementary treatments, or just a matter of coincidental timing. I always err on the side of caution with sensitive topics because specific healing effects can't be verified, and nor can we guarantee them being repeated for another individual.

Reiki *may* be able to help with fertility. I think it depends on what is causing the difficulty in conceiving. There are varying reasons why a couple may find it difficult to conceive, not least of these is dealing with past trauma or emotional stress. I have known Reiki to help heal a person on the mental and emotional level, which appeared to clear the way for them to become pregnant. When we clear our energy mentally and emotionally, it helps to bring calm to every part of us, the calm mind relaxing the body, which can be enough to clear the issue that causes difficulty in becoming pregnant.

The other factor is a biological reason for being unable to conceive. We need to be honest in considering whether Reiki is likely to be able to help in this case. Let us not forget that as well as *making better*, Reiki is also *healing into wholeness*.

There are a number of medical factors that can affect women, including problems with the menstrual cycle, primary ovarian insufficiency, polycystic ovaries, endocrine disorders that affect hormonal balance, endometriosis, and growths around the uterus. Looking at these (this isn't an exhaustive list), and understanding that Reiki brings balance to the body, it's possible that Reiki can help with the issue of regulating menstrual cycles. Once we help the body to bring its own energy into balance, it isn't impossible that this helps to regulate the menstrual flow. Once a woman has a regular, healthy period, her body is in a better position to conceive. I have known Reiki to help women with their periods, but again, we can't guarantee this outcome for everyone. As Reiki brings the body into balance, hormonal imbalance issues may also be positively affected through a course of treatments, so again have a chance of increasing fertility.

Endometriosis or growths in the uterus are more difficult conditions as they are physical in nature. Reiki is unlikely to be able to reduce the growths or change the tissue growth. Therefore, I would be even more cautious in suggesting that Reiki can help in these instances, but it is possible. I myself have polycystic ovaries, and I was told by a doctor that I would find it difficult to conceive. I have been pregnant twice, without any medical help. This could be pure luck, or it could be down to regular self-Reiki.

Reiki may help to bring calm to a person's mind-state during a time that can cause great stress and upset to a couple trying to conceive. Whatever the cause of infertility, Reiki may bring a sense of peace and balance and the ability perhaps to see a clear path forward: what choices to make, what is best for them, whether they would like to try other alternative or medical treatments, and patience for these treatments to work.

Reiki may certainly complement other treatments as well, such as IVF or acupuncture. It may boost the immune system and help the body release the "happy" hormones, putting the body into a nice, relaxed state. Reiki, alongside other treatments, may heighten the chance of producing positive results. We must proceed with caution, though, and know the history of our recipient and the severity of the issue, and still manage expectations so as not to give false or certain hope.

If the desired result is produced – fantastic! We can whoop with joy in celebration for our recipient – or for ourselves – and give our thanks for the happy news.

If the difficulty in becoming pregnant isn't biomechanical, but is instead down to an unknown, then that "unknown" may be caused by emotional factors, or at the least underlying distressed emotional states could play a role. A high degree of stress, past trauma or emotional turbulence may lie at the root of such cases. In this regard, we should still gently manage expectations, but if we can work with the recipient's emotional state, helping to release pent-up emotions, healing what needs to be healed, and bring them into their present life through Reiki and letting go of what was, it may be possible to create a space in which the body relaxes, releases and prepares the right conditions to receive a baby. Once again, Reiki can work very well alongside any other treatment a client may be having, whether that's counselling, homeopathy, acupuncture or CBT.

Reiki as a complementary therapy

I keep alluding to the fact that Reiki is a complementary therapy and "works well alongside other treatments". Why then, you may wonder, bother with Reiki at all if other treatments do the actual work? Because Reiki is a wonderful therapy for relaxation, clearing the mind and bringing us into a sense of balance and harmony. Reiki can feel very subtle, but it can have a profound impact on our inner self and our mental health. It can be like a freshening breeze, blowing through every part of us, clearing out cobwebs and motes of dust that have gathered along our journey of life. Reiki is a beautiful addition to conventional or other complementary or alternative therapies, helping us mentally and emotionally, and, yes physically too.

The mental level help seems, on the surface, the most ephemeral and the least obvious, the least tangible. But consider the conversations that we are having now around mental health. It is, thankfully, much more openly discussed today. Many people sadly suffer from mental health issues, finding it difficult to keep positive and balanced or to trust their own mind. A sense of heaviness or pressure that doesn't let up, that puts criticism and worse in our minds, that continues to drip feed into our being, day after day after day. Our mental state affects our outward behaviour, dictating our actions and reactions to others. In other words, everything that we are outwardly *first begins in our mind*. This is why our mental health is so important. If we can help ourselves by bringing balance and a more positive framework in our minds, then we can go much further in helping ourselves – and others – in all ways.

It's also possible that Reiki itself can help directly with fertility and conception. It's just that we have to be careful in our expectations, because there are no guarantees with Reiki. Receiving as much help as possible through a variety of treatment methods gives us the greatest potential chance for success.

Pregnancy

Is Reiki safe to give during pregnancy? Yes! Absolutely. There are no contraindications because Reiki is simply bringing a person into holistic balance. If we think of this as akin to meditation, we can clearly see that there can't be any safety issues.

Reiki during pregnancy is not only safe, but also beneficial. It can help mum to maintain a calm mind and emotions. It can also help to soothe and minimise the physical aches and pains that come with pregnancy, as well as alleviating other related conditions. Although every individual is different, I can say from personal experience that my own in-utero babies loved it when I did self-Reiki. Particularly with my second, my son, I felt an awful lot of heat and sensations as I gave Reiki to my tummy – it was sucked right in, as if my baby was hoovering up that energy! He would wiggle and squiggle, seeming to become even more active during this time.

I do give a light-hearted warning here. Giving Reiki to an in-utero baby may have the effect of making them super-strong, healthy and incredibly active. That certainly seems to be the effect that it had on my child, although of course I can't say he wouldn't have been like this without Reiki, so please take this lightly! However, the point remains that Reiki isn't only safe, but is beneficial for both mum and baby.

Let us not forget the partner here. The mum's partner is, of course, just as important and relevant, and Reiki for the whole family is wonderful. Reiki for the partner helps them to destress, be able to relax, to take whatever it is they need during this wonderful yet potentially stressful time.

Some people today choose to have Reiki through the birth, using it as a complementary addition to their medical care. It may help to ease birthing pangs (I doubt it will ease them completely), and to deal with any other stress that may occur during this time.

Is it safe to give Reiki within the first trimester of pregnancy? This is more a matter for professional practitioners than informal family and friends Reiki. Yes, it's perfectly safe at any and all times during pregnancy. The question of treating during the first trimester is one of caution for professionals, because the first three months of a pregnancy are the most delicate – if a miscarriage happened after a person had a Reiki treatment, in their distress they may blame the practitioner. Many therapists don't treat during the first trimester, and sometimes not in the last trimester too, for this reason.

Reiki for babies

Yes, Reiki is perfectly safe for babies. One question that you may have – or get asked – is, "But babies can't give permission, so how do I stand on this from a moral perspective?"

Babies will soak up that energy if they need it. We don't need to worry about permission. If you really are worried, you can ask their spirit, on the energetic level, and you can ask for the Reiki to be for their highest good. Of course it's only going to be for their highest good as all we are doing is allowing energy to flow to bring it into balance, into harmony. If you are giving Reiki to a baby who isn't your own, I would suggest gaining permission from the parents or guardians of the baby, for their courtesy and to ensure it fits with their own beliefs.

Babies only need a short burst of Reiki, as they are so small that what is needed goes everywhere at once. We don't need to worry about the hand positions or the chakras – your giant hand will cover their whole torso, so just let Reiki flow. Every baby is as individual as we are, so each will react in their own way, but in my experience most babies react gently and positively to Reiki energy.

My own son, even before he could talk (because he had been saturated with Reiki since his conception) would grab our hands as we put him in his cot to sleep and place them over his eyes. Heat would leap from my hands. My partner and I looked at each other in wonder and say, "He's asking for Reiki!" This became a regular occurrence. When he could talk, he would say as we put him down, "Mama Reiki." Consider this: not old enough to know the mechanics of Reiki, the *knowledge* of it, but having an innate understanding of the natural *meaning* of it – a simple acceptance.

I also clearly remember one particular time when my daughter was three or four, and she was having a massive tantrum over nothing much due to being overtired, and couldn't hold her big feelings. I put my hand on her back and let Reiki flow: almost instantly her crying stopped and she calmed down. So, yes, I do believe that Reiki is beneficial for not only us as adults, to help maintain our mental and emotional state, but for our children too, right from the beginning of their lives.

It's a lovely thing to have an immediate way to help our children. Fallen down and bumped your knee? I'll give you Reiki. Are you sad? Let me give you Reiki. Feeling poorly? ... You get the idea! My son even taught his friend in the playground, when he fell down and hurt himself. My son explained, "You just put your hand there where it hurts and say Reiki on and leave it there until it feels better!" I thought this was absolutely wonderful!

On the point of saying "Reiki on" and "Reiki off" when we want to do Reiki, this isn't normally a view that I subscribe to, as I feel that Reiki is always with us, just waiting for us to open up to it. Explaining this to a young child though is a bit complex, so I used terms that I felt would be more easily understood. Now I imagine a whole class of junior school children saying, "Reiki on!" when they hurt themselves at school.

Summary

- Infertility can be caused by medical or emotional issues, and the reasons need to be considered.
- We as Reiki healers can never make any guarantees regarding treatment outcomes.
- We should be mindful of the sensitivity of this subject, and the effect our language can have on the people we are helping.
- Apparent miracles may occur and Reiki may help – but can't be guaranteed.
- Helping to bring balance and calm on the emotional and mental levels may make a positive change that also then helps on the physical level.
- Reiki is safe and beneficial during pregnancy, and for babies and children.
- Reiki is a complementary therapy; it can therefore be used alongside any other type of treatment or therapy, as well as a standalone treatment method.

18. Distant Healing

"The cosmos is within us. We are made of star-stuff. We are a way for the universe to know itself."

- Carl Sagan

Distant healing is taught at Reiki Usui level two. This is the practice of sending Reiki to someone who isn't physically present. It doesn't matter how far away they are, whether they are next door, in the next town, or halfway across the world. Reiki is energy; when we comprehend that everything is energy, we can connect with another to access Reiki for them, no matter how far away we are.

Distant Reiki is a subject that I wonder how my students are going to react to in the class. It's such an outlandish idea compared to our logical and physical everyday lives that I keep expecting someone to exclaim, "That's not possible!" But they never do. I am unceasingly amazed that the most common reaction to the explanation of distant Reiki is a simple nod and a quiet acceptance.

Some students aren't quite sure of the idea at first. However, once we have done the practical exercise - I always ask students to gain permission from a family member or friend to send Reiki to before they start their level two class - every single one understands it, and they feel more or less the same as when conducting an in-person session.

Distant Healing

My favourite method of teaching distant healing is to use a teddy bear, which is a surrogate for the absent person. Students place their hands on the teddy, going through the hand positions, thinking of the person they are sending to, and of the Reiki going through to that person. If someone doesn't wish to use a teddy, we simply visualise that person in our mind's eye, seeing ourselves with them. Again, we can physically go through the hand placements, or we can hold our hands still and just "think" Reiki, just being energetically with that person.

This is another subject within Reiki that really needs to be experienced to be understood. The idea of "beaming energy" to another doesn't sound realistic, yet it does work. Except that we are not really "beaming" energy, as Reiki is simply a connection to bring mind and body into balance. We are not "sending" energy to someone; we are turning our focus towards them and their healing.

It isn't enough to go through the mechanics – the thought of the person and the hand placements – because it's the *connection* with energy, with Reiki, that makes the difference. It's the openness of our heart and mind that is important in accessing Reiki.

I think the reason that students constantly surprise me with the simple acceptance of distant Reiki is because they have already done the groundwork at level one, accepted Reiki is energy that we open up to and connect with, and have seen, felt and experienced the wealth of benefit that this brings. Distant Reiki is just another step along that path, so, rather than seeming strange as it would to a novice, it's just another Reiki way.

This is why, I believe, distant Reiki is taught at level two. Some people have the idea that, "You can't do distant healing until you have done level two Reiki" and, "You need to be taught the Reiki symbols to do distant healing." This is a very proscribed way of thinking about it. It's the way that distant healing is taught, yes, but just because we teach it at level two doesn't mean that you can't do distant healing before then.

It's taught at level two because the amount of information that a new student takes in at level one is phenomenal: you have to get to grips with the idea of Reiki, of energy healing. You need to learn the hand positions; the meditations; why we do these. You learn the history of Reiki and its foundation. You may learn about the chakra system or the tandens, and then the practical hands-on healing, both for yourself and working on the other students, as well as having the *Reiju*. Imagine, then, if we threw in the Reiki symbols and distant healing. That would be a lot to take on board, to comprehend and assimilate in a one- or two-day workshop. Students are encouraged to *practise practise practise* after the course, to keep doing Reiki to understand it. Distant healing at level two means that the students have had time to come to know Reiki more fully, to accept it and to really understand it. When they come to level two, they are ready for these deeper teachings.

When we send distant Reiki, we use the symbol *Hon sha ze sho nen*. This has become known as the "distant symbol" and helps to "send" Reiki where we want it to go. *Hon sha ze sho nen* is often interpreted as *No past, no present, no future*; it is "the Now", hence its use in distant healing. However, it's also "I am right mind", as Frans Stiene tells us in *The Inner Heart of Reiki*. If I am in my right mind, I am in totality. I am not separate but part of the whole. All energy is one; there is no duality. Therefore I am part of everything, so of course Reiki is part of everything.

Using the symbol *Hon sha ze sho nen* helps us to focus our intention, but when we consider the intention and meaning of the symbols, can we honestly say that the symbol has the power to enact distant healing? Would distant Reiki really not work without it? Or is it simply the intention that we put into it, the concentration and the energy? Once we understand the meaning of the symbol, as with everything else we can drop it and simply be. There is more detail on the symbols in the next chapter.

Someone who already understands this concept, who accepts the idea of distant healing, may be able to perform distant Reiki prior to undertaking a level two class, and without use of the symbols. I have known several people who were able to do this, because they instinctively understood distant healing. They were ready, and they were aware. The method that we learn in class teaches us the *how* of distant Reiki, but it's our inner understanding that creates the connection with another who isn't present, and allows us to feel that Reiki between us. It's when we understand from our heart and not our head that we can truly engage with distant healing.

In traditional Reiki, students were taught to send distant healing to one person at a time. All of their energy and intention was focused on that one person. Today, people often send distant healing to several people at once, or groups of people. Healers also use a "Reiki box", into which they put the names of everyone who would like to receive Reiki. They give Reiki to the box, with the intention that every name in it receives healing. For me, this feels like a shortcut, or an abbreviated version of distant healing. By doing this, are we giving full attention to each person? Are we focused on them and our connection with them? However, this method does work for many people, and who am I to say what is right or wrong?

If something works, then it works. But I think we should also carry out distant healings in the traditional way, one person at a time, so that we can see for ourselves if there is any difference between sending to one person or to many. I do have an online Reiki group and we sometimes set up a distant healing Reiki share, where we send Reiki to one another. It is a lovely feeling, to sit in Reiki space with others, all connecting, sending and receiving at the same time. But it's also lovely, and a different feeling, to send to one person.

In my level two classes, I set my students homework. I ask them to pair up and organise a time after the class where they will send Reiki to each other when they are at home. In this way, they get to experience not only sending

Reiki to another, but also how it feels to receive distant Reiki. It can be a strange feeling and I think it's good for a student to experience this.

For the willing family and friends who agree to receive distant Reiki from the students during class, the reactions are very different. Some are not aware and don't feel anything; some are aware of something strange, like a tingling feeling or a "weird energy" around them; and some realise they feel really relaxed. A few students have said that when they got home and spoke to their Reiki receiver, that person had asked them if they sent Reiki at a certain time, as they felt "something" then, and invariably it was indeed that time we had been sending Reiki.

Some people who aren't trained in Reiki don't react to distant Reiki. This, I believe, is because they don't know what to expect, so they are not tuned in to the subtle body signs and signals. Something *could* be happening, but they are not aware enough to process those subtle signals. Other people, however, can have quite a profound reaction, feeling tingling or pulsing, or as if physical hands are resting at certain points on their body. They may find that their headache or stomach ache disappears, or their stress melts away. Some people also feel quite strange, woozy-like and light-headed.

Because these reactions can happen, I suggest we tell people when we will be sending distant Reiki, to advise them to sit or lie down in a quiet space at that time. That way the person can fully tune in to the experience, as well as being able to relax and have a time out. They are also not in the middle of driving or operating machinery when Reiki energy suddenly flows within them!

A person doesn't *have to* be sitting in a quiet space to receive Reiki. They can go about their daily business, but we should give them a little preparation if possible before-hand, in case they do have a reaction to the healing, as this could come as quite a shock if they are not expecting it. Imagine being in a work meeting giving a business presentation, and all of a sudden you start to feel tingly all over, feel like there are hands on your stomach, and your head goes light! This is why I suggest organising a time with the client or participant, so that they can choose when is best for them, and whether they want to ensure some quiet time during the session.

Someone who remains busy will still receive the healing, but they may not be fully aware of everything that happens during that time, because their awareness is on what they are doing, not how they are feeling. This is fine if it is what they want, and they may still find that they feel more relaxed afterwards.

Distant healing for the future and the past

If we accept that we can send healing to another person who isn't with us (across space) then it follows that we can also send healing to our future, and to our past (across time). How does this work? In exactly the same way: we think of the time or situation that we want to send Reiki to, and we send healing to our self in that time. Let us look at examples of the future first…

Imagine we have a job interview next week. We think we may be nervous during the interview. So we visualise ourselves in the interview, thinking about the time it will take place (*"next Wednesday at 2:00pm"*), and we send Reiki to ourselves then. This should help to keep us calm, clear-headed and grounded at that time. We can send Reiki to that time every day until the time comes, if we want to.

Or perhaps we know that we have to have a difficult conversation with someone, but we don't like dealing with conflict. We may have to confront someone over their behaviour, for example, or perhaps we have decided it's time to end a relationship. Again, we can think of ourselves having that conversation, see ourselves there, and send Reiki to our then-self. We don't even need to know the time, but just visualise the situation that we are in. Hopefully, this will help us to express ourselves clearly, to speak appropriately and to deal with whatever comes during the conversation.

Now what about the past? How can we heal something that has already happened? Well, of course we can't. What we can do is to heal the emotions and emotional baggage that *we are still carrying around inside of us because of that event.*

All of us have emotional baggage to some degree. Everything that we have been through has helped to shape us. Some of us are better at dealing with bad events in our lives than others, but we may still have bad thoughts, feelings or reactions based on certain things that have happened to us, and those thoughts and reactions can bleed into other areas of our life – the way that we deal with relationships, or how we react to criticism.

I must advise caution here. Traumatic past events may need some gentility and delicacy if we choose to focus on these, because we may still have strong reactions and associations. The goal here isn't to reawaken old wounds or nightmares, but to heal ourselves. This goes for clients too. Before we even consider wanting, with the best of intentions, to heal old trauma for a client, we must ensure this is something that they want to do and are ready to do. If it isn't somewhere that we – or our client – want to revisit, then start with something smaller and less profound.

When we are ready, and we know what it is in our past we want to heal, there are two ways to do this (actually there are a variety of ways, and you may find your own instinctive process of doing this).

The first method is gentle and simple. Sit in your Reiki meditation space. Your hands can be in your lap or on a chakra point. I like the root or the heart for this work. Say to yourself, "I send Reiki to the time when I was [age or event]. I send healing to then."

You don't need to visualise or think too hard about the particular event, but just know that you are sending healing to that time. Sit in that space, sending Reiki, for as long as you wish to. You can continue sending healing as often as you want. Gradually you may notice a shift within yourself, and certain feelings may begin to change. You may feel braver, or kinder or less angry. The memories associated with that event begin to lessen, or you find a new peace within yourself. These changes can happen immediately and in a profound way, or gradually and gently.

The second approach is a little more dynamic. Sit in the same quiet way, and this time think about or visualise the event. Please only do this *if you feel ready to face this event again*. Send Reiki to yourself in that situation. You can also see your now-self standing next to your then-self, knowing that you are no longer that person, in that space of fear or being controlled or trapped. By seeing your now-self there, you are lending your strength to your then-self, and showing that things do get better, that the situation isn't a permanent one. You can also talk to your then-self and interact with any others involved from a place of strength – from who you are now, knowing that you are no longer in their power. You may wish to give that power to your then-self, changing the story, allowing them to do or react in a way they didn't have the capacity to before, all the while continuing with Reiki.

Afterwards, you may find there are big feelings to work through. But once again a shift may well happen, profoundly or gently, changing your internal landscape in a more positive and healing way. This change may take several sessions or more for a full (or as complete as possible) healing to occur.

We can also engage in this type of healing with our clients, friends and family. We can send Reiki to the future-them, when they have a job interview or exam, and we can help to send Reiki to their past. We can guide them through this, talking and making the process an interactive one, or we can do the visualising for them, allowing the person to remain quiet and simply receive Reiki. However, we must be aware that we are not counsellors or psychiatrists, so we should tread very cautiously when doing this type of work with another. They too may have an emotional reaction afterwards, and we need to feel equipped to deal with helping them in whichever way is right at that time.

So we can see here that not only can we Reiki to keep ourselves in balance in the now, but we can help others who aren't present with us. We can help our future self or our client's future self, and we can help to heal emotions and issues that have come from our past too. Once again, follow your own instincts and intuition, explore and experiment, and find out what works for you. If this is a matter that you would like to explore, but don't feel equipped to do so by yourself, reach out to your Reiki master or a Reiki practitioner for help, support and guidance.

Summary

- We can send Reiki to someone who isn't physically present, no matter how far away they are.
- Distant Reiki is usually taught at level two, but that doesn't mean we can't send healing as a level one student.
- Understanding the concept of energy connection and putting the intention and heart into distant Reiki allows us to access distant healing.
- The symbol *Hon sha ze sho nen* is used to focus our intention to send distant healing.
- We can send Reiki to groups of people as well as to an individual.
- We can send Reiki to our future and our past, and do this for others who wish to explore this work.

19. Do The Reiki Symbols Have Power?

"We have to understand in our mind how to handle the symbols and what their real meaning is; that is what will create the power."

- Frans Stiene, 'Reiki Insights'

The symbols that are introduced in Reiki level two courses have specific meanings, and they were chosen as representations by Mikao Usui to bring the student to a deeper level of understanding.

There are traditionally four symbols taught in Usui Western Reiki, one of which is only taught at master level. Further symbols may be included from other sources such as Tibetan Reiki. Other branches of Reiki also employ additional symbols. The question, though, is: *Do any of these symbols actually hold any power?*

Well ... yes and no.

The symbols are an interesting part of Reiki, because they are used and understood in different ways today than originally intended. Initially, in the West, they were thought to be "secret and sacred", and they weren't to be shown outside of Reiki training. Any time they were put to paper, it's said that at the end of the class those papers were burned, so that the symbols couldn't be shown to others. Students had to memorise them. Then later, the symbols were published in a few books, most notably in Diane Stein's

170

A Question of Reiki

Essential Reiki, which was published in the 1980s and hugely popular. With the advent of the internet, those symbols were suddenly out there in the world. They are no longer "secret". Some may argue neither are they really sacred, though of course just as with any kind of symbol, Reiki practitioners should certainly treat them with respect.

The symbols have a visual representation and a name attached to each of them. Two of the symbols are Kanji, Japanese script, so that the "picture" is the word itself. The other two symbols have a visual representation and a separate name. The Kanji symbols are *Hon sha ze sho nen*, and the master symbol *Dai Komyo*. If these symbols are actually Japanese words, how can we call them "secret" or even "sacred"? It's like us calling the word "harmony" secret and sacred! It's the deeper meaning, the spirit behind the words, that in Reiki we tune into and try to understand. It's the teaching of the word or phrase that gives us a deeper insight.

I am not going to go in-depth in regard to each of the individual symbols here, because you will gain a more thorough understanding of these by attending a class of Reiki training. Frans Stiene's book *Inner Heart of Reiki* delves into the original meanings of these Reiki symbols, as does the excellent internet site *James Deacon's Reiki Pages* – www.aetw.org.

I often see people asking on social media which symbol "to use for protection" or "to keep away negative people". Or even, at the time of writing this during the Covid-19 pandemic, "which symbol to use to protect from the virus". The symbols aren't physical; they are not a protective shield! They don't have this kind of power. They are simply representations with meanings. To understand the symbols, let us first look at their meanings and how we use them today, and then go back to their origins…

Reiki symbols

In Usui Reiki, the first symbol that is taught is *Cho ku rei*, which is (basically but not only) drawn as a spiral. This is known as "the power symbol" as it's considered to ramp up the feel of energy and is related to physical healing. Because of its spiral shape, it was thought by some to increase the power. This may also be because *Cho ku rei* was said to be translated as "Place the power here" by Takata Sensei.

This idea of increase later became synonymous with increasing anything it was used on. So, as a misunderstanding, drawing the spiral clockwise was thought to "increase a tumour" – remember back in chapter 3 we discussed the myth of *Cho ku rei can make a tumour worse*. Of course this isn't true. The idea of *clockwise = increase and anti-clockwise = decrease* actually comes from Wiccan or earth-based traditions, which have absolutely nothing to do with Japanese teachings.

Traditionally, the symbol is drawn anti-clockwise. Some people draw it in the clockwise direction because of Western thought about the "direction of increase". If you have taken a level two class and have been taught the symbols – then use *Cho ku rei* in the way that feels right to you. Practise drawing it in your palm clockwise and then anti-clockwise. Which way feels best? If you want to follow traditional teachings, draw it anti-clockwise. But either way, and in any case, the symbol isn't going to cause harm to anyone. Let us remain rational about this: it's just a symbol. It's there to remind us to create connection. You can't cause a health scare through using the symbol!

The second symbol is *Sei he ki*, which represents balance and harmony; of bringing into wholeness. It translates roughly as "spiritual composure". It's considered to be the emotional level symbol, to help bring our emotions into balance. It's the symbol that helps with clearing and cleansing. There is only one way to draw this symbol so no confusion has grown around it.

The third symbol in Usui Reiki is *Hon sha ze sho nen*, which is written in kanji. This is the mental level symbol, to bring the mind into oneness, and it's also used during distance healings.

Finally, *Dai kyomo*, the symbol that is taught at master level, is the spiritual level symbol and translates as "the great bright light". This is also kanji, so its visual representation is the word itself.

One other symbol often taught at master level in Usui Reiki is *raku*. This is a lightning symbol and is usually only used in the attunement process.

There are more symbols in existence today that the many branches of Reiki utilise. Symbols and their meanings are used by students of Reiki according to their branch of Reiki and the teachings given. We focus on each of these symbols to gain a deeper connection to understanding Reiki energy, inside and outside.

The use of symbols today

Today, the symbols are used in a variety of different ways. They are often used in healings for others, adding an extra dimension or increased energy to that healing session: *Cho ku rei* to add more energy, or to help deal with physical pains; *Sei he ki* for emotional balance, for example. These are also used in other ways – over food and drinks; on mechanical objects such as mobile phones and cars; children's teddy bears; pet beds and blankets.

What does this do? Effectively it imbues the subject with Reiki energy, so that this is picked up by the child or the pet. For food and water, it's meant to clear toxins and increase the good stuff already in the food and drink. For mechanical objects, it's said to help fix anything on its way to breaking.

Does this work? My answer to my students is always this: "I can't tell you, you have to discover that for yourself. Try it and see. It's up to you to find out if this works or not."

Because of the specific meanings of each symbol, these are also used for: clearing a home of negative energy (*Sei he ki cleanses; Cho ku rei protects*); protecting oneself against negative energy; and imbuing crystals with positive energy. I use the term "negative energy" loosely, as what we are really talking about is old, stored energy or emotional feedback – see chapter 24 for more on this. However, I do recognise that we all have times where we feel uncomfortable, or we may have had someone in our home that brings us down or into conflict. These variations of external use weren't taught by Usui. These are a modern adaptation as students have put their own understanding (and of course cultural values) into the system of Reiki.

While change can be good (and I am not saying these uses of the symbols are wrong or ineffective, just that they aren't traditional), I think we should be careful that we don't imbue the symbol itself with the power that comes from the *intent and the meaning within the symbol*. Is it enough to draw or air draw the symbol and think we are protected? I would say, rather, that it's the *intention, attention and focus* that we put into what we are doing that creates the required condition, rather than the symbol itself. The symbol is a vehicle for our focus, rather than holding its own power.

I understand why people ask to use them as protection, either for themselves or against a virus or within the home, for example, but to truly understand the symbols we need to know their origins.

The original meanings of the symbols

The symbols came into being within the system of Reiki as another tool; a guideline to help students further develop their understanding of Reiki, just like the hands-on healing helps us to go deeper into ourselves, just as the precepts help us to focus on the mind. The symbols and their mantras – the names we associate with each symbol – are an internal visualisation: a meditation, to help us embody the meanings. They are another tool for us within our own Reiki practice and development. They were not, for Usui, external tools of power.

We can meditate on the image of each symbol, taking their meaning within, and we can also chant the names: repeating *Cho ku rei* or *Sei he ki* over and over again to achieve the same result as the visual meditation. Chanting can be a powerful tool, and one that I think isn't fully understood or utilised in our society. Most people feel quite shy about chanting because we are not taught to use our voices in such a way, so we often feel quite self-conscious. I bring the practice of chanting the symbols into my level two classes, and after the initial nervousness students realise how effective this is.

When we meditate on the symbols, either visually or through chanting, we begin to internalise their true meanings. The story of the symbols takes us on a journey. When we look at all four of the Usui symbols, we can see that we go deeper at each one – from *Cho ku rei*, physical, we connect ourselves with our body; *Sei he ki*, emotional, going to a deeper layer within and bringing calm and balance; to *Hon sha ze sho nen*, mental, going deeper yet and bringing peace to our mind; and finally, to *Dai komyo*, spiritual.

Each has layers of meaning to be looked at, contemplated and revealed to us. There are no shortcuts to this. We have to do the practices; we have to sit and do the work of the meditations and visualisations and chanting to really get this. The true understanding of the symbols as an internal meditation is a beautiful unfurling of realisation, and a journey that I love and come back to time and again. I still use the symbols in my work because I like them, but when we really *understand* them, then we can leave them behind, because we understand that *we are the symbols*, just as, when we understand Reiki, *we are Reiki*.

When we consider the symbols from this original standpoint of contemplation and meditation, does it make sense that they can "protect me from this virus?" or "stop someone from being mean to me?" We can see that what the symbols are more likely to do is to bring us into a state of harmony within our own mind and energy. It's this self-development that is likely to bring about positive changes.

It's common today for the symbols to be used when healing others, and to clear energy in our homes, so it's up to each of us to use the symbols in the way that feels comfortable for us and to take on board what feels right. We can only really do that when we understand the history and origins of the symbols, and the current cultural adaptations.

Here is the interesting thing…

Having said all that, there is still something rather fascinating about the symbols…

In my classes I ask the students to draw them on a bit of paper for practice, and then to air draw them into their hand with their other hand. Most students feel some kind of energy coming from their hands when they do this. This is before they really understand the symbols – this is at the beginning of their learning. Yet when we draw *Cho ku rei*, many students feel heat in their hands as they draw it. When they draw *Sei he ki*, they are aware of a different feel of energy than that of the *Cho ku rei* symbol. Again, this happens when air drawing *Hon sha ze sho nen*. It appears that just in drawing these symbols with our hands, we still create a sense of energy. This fascinates me: that a new student, just learning the symbols, can feel energy coming through just by air drawing them. What is happening?

Perhaps, in drawing the symbols, we are connecting with our Reiki, bringing it out with the simplicity of connection through the symbol. Or perhaps the symbols really do have an innate inner energy.

Is it only people already attuned to Reiki who can feel this though, or would a non-attuned person feel the same thing when they draw *Cho ku rei*? How or why could this happen? If we all have Reiki already, then do the symbols "ignite" that energy within us, whether we have had the Reiki attunement or not?

Because the symbols are (usually) taught at level two, you sometimes hear people say, "You can't use them at level one; you have to be trained at level two." This isn't actually true. The symbols are only taught at level two because it's another factor of understanding, of comprehension of Reiki. There is so much to take in with level one that adding the symbols on top of this could be too much for most students. We need the time to get to grips with healing, with the feel of the energy, with what it means and what it does for us.

Once we feel comfortable with that, we are ready for further information. The symbols will then make sense because we already understand Reiki as energy and its important role in healing mind and body. It isn't a physical barrier of "doing" the symbols between level one and two, but rather one of being able to comprehend the teaching of the symbols. Some people who are at level one training may well be ready and able to understand the teachings of the symbols, so I repeat: it's the attention, focus and intention that we bring to the work that has an effect on what we do.

As the quote at the beginning of this chapter says, it's the mind that creates the power with the symbols. I think that we need to be cautious that we don't attribute a sense of armour to the symbols when, really, it's our own minds and perceptions that create how we feel about something. For example, if we feel we need to protect ourselves from someone's energy, can we use our own inner strength to do this, rather than a ritual of particular symbols? If we feel we need to cleanse ourselves energetically, can we *be* that cleansing process rather than having to use *Sei he ki*?

The symbols are something that many students tend to leave by the wayside after their training course, perhaps unconsciously thinking that these aren't as important as the hands-on healing. Certainly in the West, the hands-on element appears to be the most important, because it's practical and we can see and feel the results from it, such as heat and sensations in our hands and bodies, and we receive feedback when healing others. But the symbols are just as much Reiki as hands-on healing. All of the elements within the system are just as important as each other, and we gain so much more insight and depth if we incorporate and focus on every aspect, instead of just one.

Take time to meditate with these symbols (if you have taken a Reiki level two class). Visualise them, chant them and contemplate their in-depth meaning. Use them for yourself and with others during healings. See what works, how you feel and how your own personal understanding develops.

Summary

- From level two in Usui Reiki, we use certain symbols to deepen our understanding.
- These symbols are used in a variety of ways, from healings to protection and on objects. The externalised use of symbols is a modern adaptation.
- The original meanings of the symbols were for internal focus, as a tool within the system of Reiki.
- We can choose to use them externally if that feels right, and for meditation and chanting.
- Explore the uses and meanings of the symbols and see what you experience and what feels right for you.

Part IV: Practices that complement Reiki

20. The Psychic Connection

"Energy cannot be created or destroyed, it can only be changed from one form to another."

- Albert Einstein

If you have already undertaken your Reiki training, were there people in your class who started talking about seeing spirits (ghosts)? Or what they can "naturally pick up" from others? Did they start talking about understanding a person's past or past life? Did they say that overnight, after the attunement process, their dreams were really vivid and full of meaning? Did this make you a feel a bit uncertain, wondering if you, too, should be experiencing these things? Or did it all sound a little "woo woo" to you?

Some people are certainly genuine with their experiences, but others may feel that they have something to prove and could be embellishing or exaggerating. Either way, the psychic connection comes up a lot with Reiki. Because it's energy healing and goes beyond the physical, this can get interpreted as being part and parcel of the whole psychic scene. This sits very comfortably and naturally with some people, but not so well – or just plain nonsense – for others. The truth is, there is no right way or wrong way to how we practise Reiki.

If you don't get the whole psychic phenomena, don't worry. You don't have to get it or be psychic or open up to such experiences. This isn't a traditional part of Reiki, but something that has developed and flourished as Reiki has travelled through the "New Age" scene in North America and Europe. Let us remember that at its core Reiki is very simple: hands on, heal!

No, you don't have to be psychic to practise Reiki. No, it isn't expected that you see or feel spirits, ghosts, beings, aliens, angels etc. No, you don't have to see or feel a person's past or what they have been through, or indeed their past lives. None of this is connected to the simple system of Reiki. Don't panic if it doesn't happen to you, isn't in your belief system, or isn't something you are interested in. Practise Reiki in the way that feels right to you.

If, however, you are someone who does connect with psychic elements, that is fine too. Reiki helps us to brush aside distractions, go deeper within ourselves and connect to more than the physical, which may open up the pathway of our psychic self. I have had students say that their psychic abilities grew stronger after receiving the Reiki attunement, or when practising with Reiki. I have had students say that they remember having psychic experiences as a child, but that it had gone long ago, and reopened again after their *Reiju*. Reiki certainly can interrelate with psychic awareness, for someone already on this path and with these beliefs, because it can help us open up our intuition, our own deeper awareness. If this is something we are already connected to, we may simply become more aware of these abilities and these experiences.

Psychic abilities and experiences can take a number of forms. These include:

- seeing, hearing or being aware of ghosts (passed on spirits)
- seeing instances of the past in another person's life

- getting a sense or awareness of a person's past life
- "knowing" things you haven't been told
- dream predictions – i.e. dreaming about something and it comes true

Having a belief in psychic phenomena isn't binary, but rather, is a spectrum. We may be open to believing some things but draw the line at others. For example, we may be happy to believe in the feel and sight of auras, but draw away from the idea of the fifth dimension. We may want to work with angels or spirit guides, but don't have any time for past lives. Each of us will have our own collection of ideas in this regard.

Being open and aware of such abilities can be a joy and a wonder to work with, but we should also be cautious, and constantly analyse ourselves to ensure that what we are experiencing really is an external phenomenon. Sometimes, our own minds can be very eager to please and present logical assumptions to us, rather than what we are seeing in our mind's eye really relating to our recipient. Just because we think something about someone doesn't mean it's true – it could just be our mind presenting its own idea to us.

It's very easy to trick ourselves into thinking that something our own mind has created through imagination is actually true. Therefore, we need to understand how to regulate our self and know whether our experience is genuine, rather than being the product of an overactive imagination. This may sound strange, but it does happen. I am not saying that having a psychic awareness doesn't happen, but just that we need to be able to tell the difference and be prepared to examine ourselves honestly, differentiating between a true psychic experience and an overeager ready-to-please mind!

It sometimes happens that people who don't expect to have any psychic abilities find themselves having this experience. This can be overwhelming.

The sudden influx of ephemeral information, visions or sounds can come as a shock, and it can be too much to cope with. "How do I turn this down/off?" is a question that I get asked on a regular basis.

If this happens to you, and it isn't something that you feel ready for, the simplest method is best. Ask the universe (or the divine, or the conscious will, or spirit – whatever you want to name it) to tone it down, or off. Explain that you are not ready, or that it's too much, or that it makes you uncomfortable. This may sound a little strange, but it does work.

So be open to psychic experiences, or don't be. Either way is fine. Don't feel left out if you don't want to go down this path, as it isn't expected nor is it a requirement of a Reiki healer.

Now we come to healing others and the psychic connection. Our recipients fall into two categories: just like us as healers, they either enjoy and want to engage with psychic phenomena, or it isn't on their radar and isn't something they are comfortable with or have time for. We need to manage their expectations and let them know what to expect with us as a Reiki healer or practitioner.

Firstly, let us explore the client who does believe in psychic occurrences. At least once in your Reiki life when working with others, you will come across a person who says to you afterwards, "So what did you see?" or "What did you pick up?" or "What is it in my past that has caused my blockage?" If people come to Reiki without knowing too much about it, there is a feeling of Reiki being synonymous with being psychic. Our answer to this question depends entirely on what kind of healer we are.

We can mitigate this prior to the session by explaining exactly what Reiki is and what it does. If a person mentions wanting to connect with a loved one who passed on or expects us to pick up something from their past, we can gently explain that this isn't what Reiki is and not how we work, if we are a non-psychic Reiki healer. We can tell them what they can expect from us and from Reiki. Most people are completely satisfied once they have a better understanding.

If this hasn't been discussed prior to the treatment, and our recipient asks this question afterwards, as a non-psychic healer we need to explain to them that we don't work in that way, and it isn't what our job is. Then we can say what we did feel during the session, in terms of energy balance. We can discuss the areas where we felt more heat or sensations and what that may signify, physically, emotionally or energetically. We can also ask them what they felt during the session, and how they feel now, afterwards. This is the important factor in doing the treatment after all.

If, on the other hand, we are a psychic healer, we can answer the question of "What did you pick up?" We may well have experienced something over and above Reiki, whether that is another spirit nearby, something about the person's life, or intuition as to why they are experiencing their current issue. But we should clarify to the client that this is something alongside Reiki. If we don't make this distinction, if that client ever has Reiki with someone else, they may expect to have a similar experience, which would be unfair for both them and the next Reiki healer.

We should also be aware of whether our discussion with our recipient is appropriate. Just because we may experience something or pick up some information, this doesn't mean we have to tell them everything about it. Is it appropriate? Could it be emotional? We should always be aware of the client's needs and their emotional state. Some healers can be too eager and start chatting away about things that can cause shock or self-doubt in a client, leaving them in a potentially vulnerable state after the session.

Other Reiki healers and I have come across this with clients: people who have had a bad experience, not with Reiki itself, but the treatment from an unwise or unaware Reiki practitioner who has told them things without explaining or clarifying what they mean, or who have touched on past events or traumatic experiences. This understandably can make them feel nervous and wary if they do choose to try Reiki again. Be aware of the person as a whole, not just their desire for a psychic experience, and be certain that your ego isn't trying to play a part either.

On more than one occasion, I have had a client say to me, "I went to a psychic and she/he told me that…"

"Yes," I say, "but how do you feel about it?"

"What?" they say. "What do you mean?"

"Well, a psychic may have told you that, but does it feel true to you? What do you think about it?"

I explain that psychics are people too, and all of us – healers, mediums, tarot readers, etc. – also come from a place with our own experiences, judgements and assumptions. We see through the coloured lenses of our own experiences. Just because we *tell* a person something doesn't make it true. Many of our experiences are open to interpretation, and there can be several variables involved. Let us not forget that although there are genuine people out there willing to help others through their natural abilities, these arts are sadly peppered with charlatans. Therefore, for me, any of us can suggest things to people, but can we really tell them an absolute? Should we take as gospel the word of a psychic, medium or healer? Caution and reason should always be by our side in these matters.

"Just because I tell you something," I tell my client, "doesn't necessarily mean it's true. It's my interpretation, a suggestion only. It's up to you whether to take it on board or chuck it out the window."

We have to be so cautious when dealing with other people, because we don't know their experiences, or what they may do with information that "comes through". We don't know how they will take it, or what effect it will have on them. This is someone's life. Their feelings, their trust … their emotions. We should always remember that.

I once had a very personal experience with a client during a session. I felt a "being" at my side, literally jumping up and down for attention. I knew what this being was and what it wanted. No, this doesn't happen often, and no, it isn't something that I consciously bring into my Reiki sessions unless I have had that discussion with the client first. But this popped up of its own accord.

As my client was a person I had come to know very well indeed, we had already had many personal and spiritual discussions. I suspect that if this was a new client I was seeing, this sudden apparition wouldn't have appeared. If it did, I probably wouldn't have done anything about it, so as not to scare the daylights out of said client. In this situation though, being familiar with this particular person and trusting my intuition, I chose to mention the situation to her and ask her if she was ready to do some deeper work. We both attended to this being and what it represented, and the session went very well, creating a pathway to a deeper healing for the client.

In this case I had to make a judgement, and that judgement was easy because of my familiarity with this client. In another situation, my judgement may have been a different one.

We should also be very aware of people who come eagerly to their Reiki sessions expecting something to happen every time, like those who go to a medium on a weekly or monthly basis. Some people can become dependent on mystical information, which doesn't help them live with the reality of their life. We shouldn't lead people to expect something psychic to happen every time – because we simply don't know what may happen session to session. Even as a Reiki healer who works in the psychic field, we also need to be aware of an over eagerness in ourselves, feeling that we need to prove something to a client. Yes, this can and does happen too: desperately wanting to pick something up, or have a psychic experience, to prove to the client that we are genuine. There's nothing to prove. When we truly understand what Reiki is, there's no need for anything else. Just trust. Trust in yourself, and in Reiki. Psychic experiences happen in their own way and time. It isn't something that we can guarantee, so we shouldn't feel like a failure if no psychic phenomenon occurs.

Then we have the other type of client – someone who has no belief or need for a psychic experience. What should you do in this case as a psychic healer? One of the questions that I may broach in the initial discussion with a client is their belief system, gently asking or finding out about their beliefs to help me understand the best way to talk to that person. This is often brought through in their language and the questions they ask, or their responses to my questions.

I don't explicitly ask, "What is your religion?" or "Do you believe in ghosts?" The discussion is more subtle than that, but those who have alternative beliefs often jump at the chance to discuss angels or loved ones who have passed on, and similar. In which case we can happily discuss such things with them. But for those who are very down to earth with no such belief, even if I believe or may feel that angels are present, I am not about to start babbling this to them as it's only going to make them feel uncomfortable, think that I am strange, and unlikely to come back for another session!

As a psychic healer with this type of client, it's best simply to keep the session to straightforward Reiki. Even if you do have a psychic experience, is it appropriate to discuss it with this person? In this case, it may be best to say nothing. Of course, each person is different and they may be open to listening. Only your judgement will determine this. But if you start talking about the "woo woo" stuff before assessing the person and situation, you may end up never seeing them again. It could be that after the first session or two, once they have had a chance to absorb and process what has happened, an individual begins to open up, gaining an interest in the "weird stuff", and you can start discussing details that perhaps they wouldn't have been open to at the beginning.

Each situation needs to be judged according to its own experience. We need to look after our recipient first and foremost, managing their needs and expectations. We must work according to our own way of being, being open and flexible enough to talk to each person in terms that also make sense to them.

Whether we are psychic, partially psychic or into some forms of "woo woo" but not others, or we are completely practical and straightforward, is absolutely fine. We should be respectful of each other and understand that we all have different beliefs and our own perceptions and perspective on Reiki. Being psychic or having a psychic experience doesn't make someone a better healer, or more powerful or more spiritual. It's just another way that some people perceive life.

A Reiki session pure and simple is just as effective and just as relaxing and beautiful on its own terms. There are times when this is actually the best course to take with someone: strip everything else away and just be, in that moment with the client and the feel of Reiki, creating a simplicity and calm that is beneficial with a feeling of support for a client. There are many people who like (and indeed, can prefer) the simplicity of "just Reiki". Being able to step out of the way of ego, and to understand that pure connection with whatever it is that we call Reiki (energy / essence / Divine will / Balance…) is a skill. It's this as much as anything else that takes the time, patience and practice to learn and to understand. There are no shortcuts to this. Adding other parts to Reiki, such as the psychic experience, is just that: an added extra, a way that some people work, but it doesn't and can't shortcut the understanding at the heart of what Reiki is.

Summary

- Being psychic isn't a requirement of being a Reiki healer.
- Psychic abilities can work wonderfully alongside Reiki.
- Reiki can help any psychic ability or connection to open up.
- When working with others with Reiki, we should be aware of their own beliefs and expectations and work to manage these.

- We can talk with a client or recipient about any psychic experience that we have with them during a treatment if that person shares a belief in certain non-physical phenomena.
- We should be aware that not everyone shares these beliefs; even if we are a psychic, it may be best not to discuss anything that we experience.
- We should always be aware of self-examination, ensuring any psychic experience is genuine and not an over eagerness of the mind on our part.
- It's perfectly fine to work simply with Reiki, and to not have any psychic beliefs or experiences.

21. Seeing Colours, Auras And Energy

> "...with an eye made quiet by the power
> Of harmony, and the deep power of joy,
> We see into the life of things."

- William Wordsworth

"Should I see colours when working with Reiki?"
"How do I see auras?"
"How should I be seeing the energy?"

Just like the concept of psychic abilities, there seems to be an emphasis on being able to see the colours of auras or energy. This is fine if we naturally see them, but we don't have to, to be real or to be effective with Reiki. It's a wonderful skill to have, and some people can learn to do this with training exercises. Others don't or can't see energetic colours, and don't feel the need to.

I think the pervasiveness of this idea comes from that root of wanting to prove something tangible and definite to the recipient, as Reiki itself can at times feel subtle and vague. Being able to say to someone, "Oh, I see yellow and orange around you, and it's a bit darker here, representing some stuck energy…" somehow feels more definitive. Yet we don't need to do this. If we are comfortable with Reiki, and we have set our boundaries at the beginning with the client explaining what they can expect during our session together, then they will be perfectly satisfied and their expectations will be managed. We have absolutely nothing to prove, not to the recipient and not to ourselves.

Even after all this time, I don't see auras. But I do, at times, sense them. I *feel* them, like a knowing. This is a little difficult, because how can I prove this? It comes from a place of self-trust, of knowing myself well enough to understand all the little signals that happen within, and how to listen with all of my senses to what is going on. Each of us is different. Some people may "see" colours, auras or the energy, and some, like me, may sense or feel them. Others may "hear" them – they may cause a different vibration per colour, or they may hear it as a whisper in their ear. So just because you don't see energy doesn't mean you are not picking up on something.

Be aware of all your subtle senses. This is a skill or ability that can't be rushed. Time, patience and practice may see your awareness open up. As ever with Reiki, it doesn't always happen and can't be guaranteed to happen every time. Sometimes, when I am working on someone, I will look down and occasionally see a little flash of blue. I hope it happens again and I watch closely, but it never does. It only happens when I am in the moment, when I am not in my head space, thinking or holding any expectation. Because I am not expecting it, I am open, in awareness, in *Reiki*, so I see and experience what there is to see and experience.

This is the paradox of Reiki: to have no expectations – to surrender. When we stop trying, we experience. Even though I don't see auras, I can talk to clients about the sensations, about where I felt heat or tingling more strongly and what that may represent, where they feel balanced, and how the whole session felt: gentle, calm, peaceful or grounding, earthing energy or moving energy from head to heart. These discussions are wonderful and often help the client to understand what is going on with them, either on the surface or at a deeper level.

"Yes," they'll say, "I've been too much in my head, and not grounded enough. I definitely feel more grounded now!"

Or, "That felt so protective, like someone was gently holding me in their arms and telling me everything is okay."

For me, this is enough. I do see colours in my mind, and if something is particularly strong, I will talk this through with the client to check if it has any meaning for them. More often than not, we see or feel the same colours. We will agree on blue-greens and a sense of water, or yellow and oranges and healing at the sacral chakra or at the emotional level. I always ask the client to take from these discussions what is right for them, though, and not just to take my word for it. I like to discuss things *with* clients, to get their feedback and thoughts, so that they are empowered and part of the session, with their own understanding of the process and the healing.

Students of Reiki, as well as clients, ask me about the meanings of the colours we see during a session. My answer is that they can have several meanings, or none: don't get hung up on a definitive meaning, because seeing colours and auras isn't the point of Reiki. How a person feels *after* the session is the point ... whether Reiki helps them to feel better in any way. The rest – the colours, psychic connection, guides and spirits – is essentially paraphernalia. They are added extras, which can be wonderful and helpful, but they are not the *essence* of Reiki.

The meaning of colours is often connected to the chakras: seeing colours can tell us which energy centres are operating strongly or are taking the most healing. Each chakra is associated with a particular colour, so the colours that we see can give us an indication of what is happening at that chakra level. However, this may not be the case. The colours might instead be linked to our emotions, and that definition actually depends on our own individual association with colour. For example, most people associate yellow with happiness; red with anger; purple for psychic or intuition; green for healing, and so on. We should be aware though that this doesn't apply to everyone, so we need to explore the options with a client. Which emotion do they associate with white, blue or orange, for example? Do they feel that there is a reason why they, we or both of us, saw a given colour so strongly? How do they feel about this?

By all means, we can give them our suggestions and interpretations, and it's then up to the client to decide whether that makes sense to them. Colours may also be connected to angels, earth or heavenly energy, or the elements of fire / earth / water / air, depending on how the session is going, our beliefs, the client's needs, and so on. So there is no singular definition of "seeing colours". This can seem complex and confusing, but it's often the case with any type of energy work that there's no absolute definition! This is why we need to be open and not be so narrow in our focus or expectations, and simply accept the experiences as they arise. Only time and patience and discussion, and the experience itself, will help us to determine the most suitable assessment of a particular session.

Auras are healthy and balanced if we see them as a bright colour, and even (rounded and uniform) in shape. They may contain several colours, indicating different feelings or energy around that person. Any darkness of colour, such as a dull orange, muddy pink or black, is likely to indicate that the energetic level of that person needs some healing, as can a sense of jaggedness or sharpness to the aura. Some healers feel or sense this rather than seeing it in terms of colours.

When conducting a Reiki session, if we have our hands off a person, we could possibly feel where their aura extends to – that is, how far from their body their auric field stretches. If it's quite far out from their body, this can indicate that they are too open and are taking on outside information, i.e. the energetic impact of other people. Giving Reiki to the aura field can help to bring this back into balance and to rest where it should naturally be around that person. There are books and information on the internet that can provide practices to help you see auras and colours, if this is something that you would like to explore further.

Seeing Colours, Auras And Energy

This is one of the many reasons that I love Reiki so much: that it's so simple at its core. Reiki is for everyone, whatever our background, beliefs, religion, experience or ability. All we need to do is be willing to open ourselves to that connection. Reiki is also adaptable, versatile and happy to work with other strands that blend so well with it ... whether that is in the form of physical treatments such as massage or reflexology, other energy practices such as aura readings or shamanic work, or seeing spiritual beings. It's so flexible and adaptable that no one, no belief system, no way of working, is excluded. If we are simple, traditionalist and no nonsense, we can work with Reiki. If we are psychic, we can work with Reiki. If we see auras, we can work with Reiki. Whoever we are, and however we like to work, we can work with Reiki. We *are* Reiki.

Summary

- Many people ask about being able to see auras, colours or energy with Reiki.
- This isn't something we have to be able to do as Reiki healers but we can add it to the work if we want to.
- Some healers naturally see auras and energy colours – this is also fine.
- Even when we do see auras or energy colours, this isn't the point of Reiki, and we shouldn't get hung up on meanings or definitions.
- The essence of Reiki is the simple experience of it, and how we or our recipient feel afterwards.
- Books and website information about how to see auras can be helpful.
- The colours that we see in Reiki can have many different meanings, and we should discuss these with our recipient but be cautious about telling them what the colours mean.

- Reiki is so beautifully adaptable that it can work wonderfully on its own as pure, simple Reiki, or alongside and with other physical treatments, aura seeings, colours, guides, angels etc.

22. A Question Of Spirit Beings, Reiki And The Shamanic Connection

"Shamanism is a path of knowledge, not of faith, and that knowledge cannot come from me or anyone else in this reality. To acquire that knowledge, including the knowledge of the reality of the spirits, it is necessary to step through the shaman's doorway and acquire empirical evidence."

- *Michael Harner*

Angels and spirit guides are another part of the "modern era" of Reiki. It was not, as far as we are aware, part of Mikao Usui's traditional Reiki teachings. The idea of shamanism and Reiki, however, is more of a fluid area, as we shall see.

I often find myself thinking of Mikao Usui whenever a question comes up about Reiki: what would he think about this? Could he envision this as a part of Reiki? In the book Reiki Shamanism, Jim Pathfinder Ewing asserts that he believes that Usui was indeed a shaman:

"The way in which people are treated using the hands, not for physical manipulation, but for guiding energy, transmitting energy, breaking energetic blockages and removing

A Question of Reiki

spiritual intrusions, is most definitely shamanic and demonstrated in other cultures, including Native American..."
(Ewing, 2008)

This point of view is contentious, and not every Reiki teacher or master agrees. However, in the traditional kanji of the word "Rei", we find the symbol for female shaman! The word "Reiki" was in use in Japan prior to Usui, but the word still became synonymous with Usui's teaching and the method of hands-on healing, so is there a clue in this? We know comparatively little about Usui and his own training and beliefs. We know that he was a Buddhist priest and undertook certain training methods, including fasting and meditating. We know that some Buddhist branches and practices are quite esoteric. It's believed that Usui practised Shugendo (Stiene and Stiene, 2010), and that this spiritual training included shamanic practices, as well as Buddhist and Taoist. We also know that in Japanese culture, particularly from Shintoism, there is an ingrained belief in protective spirits:

"The Hakuryuujin, which consist of a male and a female dragon ... have been protecting my family for more than 2000 years."
(Yamaguchi and Petter, 2008)

While we can't know for certain how traditional teachers would have got on with the idea of angels or guardian spirits, it seems that it wouldn't necessarily have been outside of Usui Sensei's own beliefs. How would he feel with the idea of spirits being interrelated with Reiki? I suppose we will never know. I recognise that anything that is going to continue to survive must adapt, but I also have a deep respect for the traditions that brought Reiki into being as we know it today. To truly understand anything, we gain much by knowing its roots: where it came from, why, and the traditions and cultural understanding surrounding it. So much risks becoming lost when something is cut off from its roots.

So on this point I say, "What is right for you? What feels right to you with Reiki? *There is no right way, there is just your own way.*"

I think that new students in particular struggle with this. It's a topic I see coming up a lot on social media:

- "I see a lot of people talking about angels. How do I do this?"
- "I completed my Reiki level one x months ago and haven't seen any angels yet?"
- "Am I doing it wrong as I can't seem to connect with my spirit guide?"

As I have reiterated throughout this book, it's perfectly valid to be "just Reiki", without bringing in other non-corporeal phenomena. It isn't fair for people on social media forums to tell others, "You have to connect with your guide" or "You are doing it wrong if you haven't found your angel." This isn't a path for everyone, and these experiences are an additional tool alongside Reiki. It doesn't matter one jot when or if you connect with any kind of spiritual being. Even if it's something that you would like to incorporate, it's going to take time and work and patience for this to happen. It doesn't affect our connection with Reiki, or the way that we treat others.

Just as Reiki complements medical treatments and other holistic therapies such as reflexology and massage, and isn't either of these but works gently with them to boost the effects that they bring, so too does it work alongside the psychic and non-corporeal realm. Reiki is Reiki: holistic healing by connecting with universal *ki*. But what does it actually mean to connect with angels, guides or spirit beings?

Animal guardians – and the connection with shamanism

Animal guardians, guides or spirits are non-physical beings that can come and join us to be our personal friend, a protector and helper, as well as assist in our healing work. The idea of an animal guide or guardian has been present in many different native cultures, from the ancient Celts to the tribes of the Native Americans, to the Aboriginal peoples. These guardians may choose to help us in our healing work – not every spirit animal does, they each have their own role – and may help us by informing us about what needs healing, or what is the root cause of the issue that we are working on. Or they may simply do their own work, lending their energy to the session.

The experiences differ from person to person, spirit animal to spirit animal, and session to session. If and when they first appear to us, it's usually for us to learn from and with them about our own self, quite similar actually to how we start with Reiki. We need to do the personal self-work first to gain the true and deeper understanding of what we are doing and the relationship that is forming. If we spend time with our spirit animal first, asking questions, experiencing the connection, their role with us, and what we can learn from them about our own journey and self, our relationship with them becomes stronger. We will then have a greater understanding of their energy and help if and when they choose to assist us during our healing sessions or in other ways.

Animal spirit guides and guardians are actually a crossover from the shamanic world. Really and truly, working with any type of spiritual being comes from shamanism. This is where it all began; the belief that all things are energy and have a spirit, and that spirits exist without form.

It bamboozles me, I must admit, when I see comments online by people who are adamant that Reiki has nothing to do with shamanism, but then proudly declare that they work with a guardian angel or a spirit being. I think some people have a very narrow view of what "shamanism" means, and perhaps for some in the West it conjures ideas of dark or crazy magic. This isn't at all true. Shamanism is a living, breathing concept beyond religion and religious belief, just like Reiki. It's animistic, a belief that every living thing – including mountains, rocks, streams and plants – has its own spirit. Shamans, or shamanic practitioners, are able to communicate with spirit beings and bring back to the real world answers about life, healing, purpose, and much more.

Shamanism spans time and cultures. Siberians, Finns and the Sami, Aboriginal peoples, North American tribes and African tribes people all had (and have) shamanic cultures, showing that shamanism isn't one homogeneous belief or religion, but a set of beliefs that share a commonality, even though these are practised in very different ways in each tribe and culture. Many of our stories in Europe are rooted in shamanism, even though we may not be aware of it (having a protective guardian; travelling through magic holes or doors). It's about drumming to induce trance states and commune with the spirits, dream-walking, and seeing "beyond". No, we don't have to practise shamanism to have a spirit guardian or animal guide, but shamanism is the root of where this idea originates.

"A shaman would say that it is dangerous not to know about shamanism. In ignorance of shamanic principles, people do not know how to shield themselves from hostile energy intrusions through having guardian spirit power."
(Harner, 1990)

For me, Reiki and shamanism are like two separate trees that grow together: they have their own separate strands, but they are friends and do well when their branches intertwine. Japanese Shintoism is shamanic, or at least animistic, with its belief in *Kami* – spirits.

What then is the difference between shamanism and Reiki? Reiki can remain very practical: hands on – let it flow! Let the energy be, *Just Be*. We

A Question of Reiki

can add the colours, spirit guides, angels and intuitive information to this – which for me is the crossover that blends to and from shamanic work. Shamanic work, however, is deeper, more involved and more dynamic, where the healer or shamanic practitioner enters trance states to journey to the spirit realms to find answers, and consciously works with spirit beings, among other things.

I am a shamanic practitioner as well as a Reiki practitioner and teacher. I drum, I "journey" and I talk with spirits. Yet when it comes to Reiki, I naturally keep the two practices separate. I don't consciously bring the shamanic element into my Reiki work, unless it arises naturally. I am quite a practical person and, yes, I have beliefs in things that many people find outlandish, but I won't immediately assume that everything that happens in my life or for a client is the consequence of a magical experience. I look for rational causes first. In other words, I am grounded. I walk the middle path, understanding both the real world in front of us and the world we can't see with our own eyes.

I understand that some people are not prepared to believe in the existence of "other", so bringing this into Reiki sessions would serve no purpose for them. I help people in the way that is right for them. Sometimes, though, people ask me about deeper work, and then we discuss the shamanic elements that can be brought in. I let this arise in its own way rather than advertising shamanic healings; people need to be prepared for this as it can be quite intense work.

Everyone has a spirit animal, if we choose to open our awareness to it. You don't need to be a shaman or shamanic practitioner, or even have a belief in shamanic practices, to connect with your spirit animal. They simply *are*, just like angels, and just like Reiki. Working with your spirit animal can teach you a lot about your own nature, development and life. The understanding and acceptance of spirit animals seems to have become a lot more pervasive in recent years, outstripping a belief or knowledge of its shamanic roots.

There are many good books and pieces of information about working with animal spirit guides. It isn't difficult to find your own if you are patient and willing to do a bit of work. Or, if you prefer, you can look for a local shamanic Reiki healer to help you through this process. Remember that not every healer may advertise themselves as a shamanic healer; if you like the look of a particular healer on social media or on their website, you can always send them an enquiry.

Angels

Angels are another form of spiritual being. They are often envisioned by people as human figures with wings, surrounded by light. This image is a very Christian concept of angels, but angels belong to many different cultures and predate Christianity. The word "angel" comes from *angelos* in Greek, meaning "messenger". It's also found in Mycenaean script, from the Greek Bronze Age. We could even argue that the Valkyries of Norse mythology are angels, as they are human in shape, with wings, and carry the worthy dead to Valhalla, the warriors' heaven. The idea of messengers from gods and angel-like beings are found in many different societies.

Some people may perceive angels as pure light or as balls of light. Angels don't take (or don't have to take) one form. Our concept of angels as human figures with wings actually comes from Renaissance paintings: this is how we have seen them in pictures, so our cultural consciousness has absorbed this image as a representation. As angels are non-physical beings, however, they can appear to us in any form. It's important to remember that what we see – or feel or experience in some way – is our mind *interpreting* what is there, in a way that it can comprehend.

Most people don't see angels physically but with their mind's eye, or they become aware of them as a comforting presence, almost a pressure against them, letting them know that another being is present. It's also worth considering that we all have different concepts and ideas. What I consider to be an angel, you may call a presence or something else: divine will, energy, love... What you, for example, call a *guiding light*, someone else may call a *protective spirit* or even *God*. When we are dealing with energy-based forms with no physical element to them, our experience is subjective, and so is the terminology that we use.

We don't need to get hung up on what has happened or what it is that is present – we don't have to define these things, or talk or think about them in absolutes. I call it an angel; you call it an energy ... it really doesn't matter. What matters, as with most things Reiki, is how we *feel* about it. Does it bring a sense of love, support and nurturing? Does it feel positive and healing? Everything else is just our minds trying to understand an undefinable concept.

Some people connect with their own personal guardian angel – a being who is specifically connected to that individual, even if it isn't present all the time but is still a protective force for that person. Some like to bring into their healing work the energy and presence of archangels such as Gabriel, Uriel, Michael and Jophiel. These beings are "higher angels". They are not directly connected to individuals, but can be invoked for their spiritual help. Some people find that generic angels appear and start helping in healings, simply because they have been asked to be present, or because they want to be. There are a variety of ways that we can ask for angelic assistance.

The fascinating thing is when we – as the healer – feel the presence of an angel and know that something amazing is happening, and then after the session our client states that they too felt an angel present, without us having said anything! This has happened in my own sessions on some rare occasions, and for both participants to be aware of such a powerful presence independently truly feels humbling.

I remember one particular occasion: I was in the middle of the Reiki treatment with a client when I suddenly felt something nearby. The presence was almost physical. I ignored it at first, because I wanted to focus on the client, but the presence made me feel that I ought to step back. "We got this," was the message that popped into my head. I really didn't want to listen, because I had no idea how the client would take this. In the end, the presence was so pervasive, so pushy, that I said to the client, "I'm just going to take my hands off you now. Just ... allow yourself to experience." Nervously I stepped back, leaving my hands open at the sides.

The presence I felt filled my mind with sunset colours of orange, gold and yellow. I have no idea how long I stood there doing nothing, letting whatever was happening happen. Afterwards the client told me that the hands-off part of the session was the most powerful for her and described wonderful sensations flowing all over her body. She reported being on quite a high for some time after that session! This experience just goes to show how we, as the healer, can't make expectations about the sessions, and nor are we always in control of them ... no attachments, no judgements ... just being with whatever occurs in that moment.

This type of experience is certainly not a regular occurrence. This doesn't happen all the time, or even often for me. I don't consciously communicate with angels, but I am open to them. They, I feel, seem to come when it's the *client* who needs them, not me. If a client requests at the beginning of the session for some help or work from angels, certainly I will open myself up and ask for angelic assistance. But if you are not someone who likes to work in this way then don't be afraid to explain that to a client. It's better to set our boundaries from the start, so that our recipient knows what to expect from us, and so that we are comfortable with our own working practice. The worst thing for you is to find yourself in a situation working in a way that doesn't fit you. If you would like to connect with angels however, there is an exercise at the end of this chapter. There are also many books out there about angels and angelic healing.

Reiki guides

What exactly is a Reiki guide? Well, that depends on who you ask, and your own perception. Generally, Reiki guides are human-form spirits that come to help with energy-healing work. They may be your own spirit guardian; a personal friend in the same way a spirit animal is. They may be more general, not specifically attached to an individual but come and go as they please, seeming to like helping with Reiki.

Reiki guides are different from angels. My own personal experience of this difference is that angels somehow feel lighter and brighter, whereas Reiki guides feel almost earthy. Some healers say that their Reiki guides are famous people who have passed, beings of ultimate compassion who share their energy healing, such as Jesus, Mother Mary or Mother Theresa. It may even be someone who isn't famous but is connected to you through your ancestor bloodlines – a great grandmother or thrice great uncle, for example – or through spirit lines, e.g. a like-minded person who shares an interest or passion with you, such as a former artist, dancer or healer.

Their presence in a healing is much the same as that of an angel: it may be someone that we see with the mind's eye, or feel the presence of, or even hear through our ears or thoughts. They may join us in the healing, adding their energy and working on the client in a different area to where we are. Or they may lend their strength or energy to what we are doing. Or yet again they may simply guide us, giving us information or helping us know where to go and why. They may not even be there for us; it's possible that they are connected to the client, or that they have come through us to help the client to heal or to protect them.

I have been aware of a presence in a handful of sessions with clients, but not known who was there; they have been blurry, indistinct to my senses. Yet they have stood sentinel over the client, as if guarding them from something. Trusting my instincts and getting no bad feelings from these beings, I have silently thanked them and left them to their work, as they left me to mine.

The most incredible sessions have been where the client stated afterwards that they were aware of a great protecting presence, without me having uttered a word. In these instances, the client and I have discussed this presence and what it could mean. In some cases, it may be that a client's personal guardian is coming through and letting them know that they – the client – are ready to connect at a deeper level. Whether they do or not, whether they explore this spiritual and esoteric connection, is up to the client.

Clients and Reiki students often report a feeling of "extra pairs of hands on me, like you were in several places at once," during a session. Some healers say that this is the presence of another being: "Oh, my Reiki guides were working with me…" and that may be true. But it may also be simply the residual feel of the energy where we have placed our hands. For example, if I have been at the solar plexus area and then move to the sacral, the person may still feel the energy at the solar plexus as if my hands were still resting there. I don't always assume that extra energy, the extra hands, are another presence. This isn't *always* the case, but in some sessions, it may well be. We can only make the distinction in each individual session.

I never feel a need to over-analyse the presence of angels or guides. The fact that they turn up is enough. Their presence is always one of comfort, peace or protection, and of love – never of fear or discomfort.

Spirit beings

We have covered angels, animal guardians and Reiki guides, so what then are spirit beings? This is a broader category and follows the same concept as angels and guides, but these can be pretty much anything else. This may include your own dear loved ones who have passed or the loved ones of the client. They may be a "messenger" guide, who comes and goes for a specific purpose, but doesn't stay attached to an individual. Some healers work with animal guides or the fairy realm, which includes elves, fairies (faeries), pixies and the like. Spirit beings may even be the spirit of the elements: fire, earth, water, air, or nature spirits such as a tree spirit. Again, these beings may be attached to us – our own personal guardian – or spirits that like to work with or through us; or they could be related to the client.

If you feel a spirit being present in your work, you may want to explore this further, through meditation, to discover their reason for coming to you. If you find it is a surprise and a shock that such a being is present, it may be a sign from them that they wish to connect with you, and that you are at some level, even if you are not conscious of it, ready to open up to this work.

I do realise that this may all seem a little far-fetched to some of you reading this book. That is fine, and you are certainly under no obligation to work in this way. But one day the sense of something "other" may appear in one of your sessions, so I hope that this information helps to prepare you just in case. It doesn't happen to everyone, nor does it need to. Yet we all have our own unique methods and beliefs, and for some of you, this concept of other beings may feel as natural as breathing.

We should all respect each other's path. I certainly feel that there is room for all of us, with all of our different ways. Clients who come to Reiki are as diverse as we are and will seek out those who share their own beliefs and can understand them.

Some of you may want to work this way but haven't had anything "weird" or "other" happen yet. I repeat what I have said before: *there are no shortcuts.* Understanding is a gradual on-going process that comes with patience and practice. When you are ready, it will happen, but you must do the work. You can't expect something to happen just because you want it to. It takes doing the self-Reiki and the meditations. Even reading books on the subject can be a help: it seems to trigger that *thing*, that essence within us, that connects us to this spiritual, non-physical world.

Summary

- Some Reiki healers work with non-physical entities, such as angels, Reiki guides and spirit beings.
- We don't need to have a belief in or work with such entities to be an effective Reiki healer.
- This kind of work could have been a part of Usui-Sensei's belief system, as there are esoteric branches of Buddhism and Shintoism.
- The connection with such non-physical beings has its roots in Shamanism, which is a living belief system and practice that spans cultures and time.
- Angels, Reiki guides and spirit beings can be connected to us, or to the client, or choose to join in a healing just because.
- Each of us experiences these non-physical beings in our own way, depending on our own past experiences and our belief systems.
- We need to take the client's needs into account: if they don't believe in such phenomena, it isn't going to mean much to them, or to be helpful, to talk about spirit guides.
- We need patience and time to connect with our own guides, angels and guardians, and can learn to do this through our own self development work, including meditations and Reiki.
- We can read books on the subject, and even seek out a mentor, such as a shamanic Reiki healer to help us find and connect with our own guides.
- Observe and be open if any such experience happens to you during a healing session; allow your mind, heart and spirit to be open and aware of whatever may happen and any information that may come through.

Exercise: How to connect with angels

I haven't included an exercise on connecting with your animal guide as this work has the potential for deep and emotional impacts. It's better to do this in a supported way, in a group or with a mentor, who can help and support you through the journey. There are books and online articles that deal with animal guides, and it's up to you if you choose to find your own animal guide in this way. It can be an enormously rewarding experience and isn't difficult for many people. However, we never know the impact of such energetic work, so I ask that you proceed with preparation and awareness.

Make sure that you are alone, in a quiet space and time, and are not going to be disturbed (switch your phone off!).

Light a candle. You can choose to play some gentle background music if you wish, light some incense and have crystals around you (not necessary, but it can feel nice).

Sit comfortably and take some time to go into yourself. Relax, and let all thoughts of the day and all distractions leave your mind. This may take some time, so be patient.

When you feel calm inside, think about angels and connecting with angels. Think in whichever way is right for you: in mere thoughts or visualising angels. What or how you visualise doesn't matter: just whatever comes and what is right for you.

When you are ready, say to yourself, out loud or quietly, "I am ready to connect with angels [or 'my personal guardian angel'… whichever way you wish to connect at this time], I am open, please come, be with me, let me know you are here."

Remain quiet and open, receptive in heart and spirit. It may take some time. An angel may come physically – you may see a ball of light, or colours, or something else unusual, or you may see them vividly in your mind's eye – or you may feel a sudden presence, almost physical, or a sensation, such as a sudden rush of love or openness, or something else very positive. You will *know*.

When this happens, thank them for coming to you. Take some time with them. Which type of angel are they? Are they your personal guardian, or other? What can you learn from them? What is the best way for you to connect with them? Can they help you with healing or something else? Do they have a name? If this feels too much at this time – if you felt overwhelmed at their presence – leave it there and do this part at another time.

Stay in this moment for as long as you wish. When you are ready, gently return to the real world. Make sure you are back fully by concentrating on your body (the feel of it) and your breathing.

If nothing happens, don't worry. It may be that you will dream and your dreams will reveal something. Or something may happen the next day or the day after. Don't be discouraged, as you can always try again. It may take several tries (or more). Not because the angels aren't there or don't want to work with you, but because – just like with Reiki – it may take time to get your conscious mind out of the way and be open to hearing, seeing or sensing the non-physical.

Once you have found that connection with angels, feel free to go back and have conversations with them.
- "How can I heal myself?"
- "Can you help me to heal from…"
- "I'm feeling vulnerable right now, can you protect me?"

No question is too silly! You will receive an answer about whether they can be of help in certain ways. Some may be willing to help in your healing work, but just as with other spiritual beings, each angel is different and may do or not do certain things i.e. healings, protection, etc.

Please do be aware, though, that they will do what is *right* at that time, not necessarily *what you think you want*! Don't expect to win the lottery because you have an angel at your side. And don't be dependent on them to fix every problem you have. How can you grow as a human being, how can you learn who you are and what you are capable of, if your angel, or other spiritual friend, fixes all of your problems?

The sense and feel of an angel, or indeed other spiritual ally, will *always* be one of love, or protection, or positive in some way. It will never feel uncomfortable or *dark*.

23. Psychic Attacks And Spirit Intrusions

"Face the sunshine, and your shadow will fall behind you."

- Old adage

Experiencing a psychic attack or dealing with spirit intrusions is definitely outside of the traditional teachings, but it's something that you may encounter in modern Reiki.

What is a spirit intrusion? If we accept the fact that benign spiritual beings such as animal guardians and angels exist, then it follows that there are also spiritual beings or forms of energy that aren't so friendly to us. This doesn't mean that they are bad or evil per se, but think of them rather as not compatible with the human form.

Through certain circumstances, *which are incredibly rare*, someone may feel that a spirit energy has intruded into their own – an energy that isn't part of that person and isn't compatible with them. This isn't going to happen in any way with the straightforward Reiki work that we do. Even engaging with friendly spiritual beings only happens if we invite them, choose to work with them, or are ready even at an unconscious level to see and feel them.

> "...shamanic practitioners view intrusions as energies directed to us by malevolent, alien or unconscious external forces. This could be objects embedded in us from past life wounds or as disassociated emotions, thoughts, and feelings congesting as tangible shapes and forms in spiritual reality."
>
> (Roberts-Herrick and Levy, 2008)

When we are doing Reiki for ourselves, there is no question that it's spiritual energy – or essence – and that we are healing through our connection to this universal energy. That is it – nothing bad can come through, there can be no visitations of bad spirits, ghouls, ghosts or other. When we are giving Reiki to another, all we are doing is helping them to align and re-balance in whichever way they need.

Even when sending distant Reiki, if we are simply sending Reiki to that person, just thinking of them and allowing Reiki to flow to and for them, we can't come under an energetic attack of any kind. *Reiki doesn't invite any type of negative energy, spirit intrusion or attachment.* It's balance, alignment, compassion, and/or working with a force or a field of essence that is just there.

People sometimes believe that they already have a spirit intrusion attached to them, or that they have come under a psychic attack. So what do we, as healers, do in this case? We may come across such experiences during the course of our healing work, but I think that we do need to be cautious in this. As more people are aware of this phenomenon, it's another almost "cool" experience to have. It's so easy to say, "I have a spirit attachment that I want to let go of," or "I'm under a psychic attack and I need to clear it!"

Each case should be dealt with on its own individual merit. I wouldn't assume that just because a client or a friend says and believes such a thing, it's necessarily true. People who are going through a really difficult time, are feeling emotionally disturbed, or are under a lot of stress, for example, could attribute general bad luck or emotional down days to something more esoteric and spirit-like happening to them. It may, for some people, be easier to attribute a reason for their current bad luck or stressful situation, rather than just life being what it is at that time. So, if someone says to you, "I have a spirit attachment and it's horrible!" you don't have to take their word for it – keep an open mind, considering that this may or may not be true.

I understand that this topic isn't for everyone and is a little too "way out there" for some. This is absolutely fine, but I hope that this gives you some useful information if you ever do find yourself encountering such an event.

I have had personal experience of a spirit entity attachment. Some years ago, I was conducting a shamanic healing for someone, before I had a true understanding of the safety structure of shamanic work. During the healing, I encountered a spirit entity, and only afterwards realised that it had attached its energy to me. I knew this because I felt off – unbalanced, off kilter and just wrong, a feeling that persisted over several days. It was only then that I made the connection with the work I had done, and both my partner and I had to work to disassociate the spirit entity's energy from me. My partner described the feel and shape of the intrusion. This was an accurate assessment even though I hadn't given him any of those details, so this confirmed my encounter.

I have learnt a lot from that experience. I now know a lot more about how to keep safe and protect myself when undertaking dynamic shamanic work. It's always advisable to set energetic protection, including an energy shield when doing more than just sending Reiki – see the next chapter for more details on this.

The understanding that entities and spirits of any kind are out there depend, of course, on your own belief system. If, however, we choose to practise Reiki in a more esoteric, non-traditional shamanic-leaning way, we may come across these entities and intrusions, so we need to know about them, how to deal with them and, importantly, how to protect ourselves.

Spirit intrusions and psychic attacks are forms of energy that are outside of our own, that don't merge or sit well with ours, and feel off or make us ill. In the case of non-friendly beings, there isn't necessarily any bad intent – they are just doing what they do, like all creatures. We are unlikely to encounter these beings unless we are journeying into the spirit world, or "Otherworld" as it's also called.

Psychic attacks are difficult to describe, because these will affect each person in a different way. Their symptoms are often the same as those with an illness such as a viral infection. There may also be a run of bad luck in someone's life, things going wrong, or an influx of sensory information – lights seeming too bright, noises too loud;, or too many people making us jittery, and so on. If we have a combination of these things, and we feel drained, unusually exhausted or constantly on edge, this could be a psychic attack. We can only know if this is the case through the use of our intuition, sensing our own energy and if we feel anything out of place, or going to a healer who has experience of dealing with energy intrusions.

I have never heard a new student or friend in my Reiki circle say that they have come across a bad spiritual entity. These occurrences are rare. As for psychic attacks, not many people know how to instigate one – and of those who do, there are even fewer who would actually do it.

In most cases of people saying that they have an attachment or are under psychic attack, it's more likely that they are experiencing the continuation of old, stored emotional habits and old energy that is no longer serving them. Or possibly the unintentional taking on of other people's energy that doesn't sit well. What they need is a good energy clearing and balancing – Reiki.

But what if we do come across a client or friend who does have an entity attachment? It's entirely up to you if you feel equipped to deal with such a phenomenon. If this doesn't make you comfortable, don't be afraid to tell the person that this isn't something that you deal with and they will need to find someone else to help. You may consider directing them to someone more experienced in these matters. Never be afraid to call on people you know in healing circles for advice and support. We all have different skills and comfort zones of what we have experienced and feel that we can deal with. However, if you do feel comfortable enough to with such an issue yourself, the following steps may help you:

- First, set protection in the form of an energetic shield (see the next chapter).
- If you like crystals, any black crystals are good for protection and warding off bad energy: tourmaline, obsidian or jet. Add any other crystals that you are drawn to. I use a selenite wand.
- Call on any spirit help – your own guardians, angels, your deity or God, whoever is right for you.
- You may wish to cast a protective circle, the area within which you will be working, infusing it with protective energy and asking your spirit helpers to help keep it protected from any harmful energy.
- Close your eyes, connect with the client and see what you feel. Trust your own senses – can you detect anything? If so, what? What does it feel like? What emotional response does it engender in you?
- The foreign energy usually enters from a particular place on the client: for example, their right shoulder, left hip, etc. You will feel a difference in energy here.
- Reiki itself seems to help weaken or clear any spirit or attachments. This can be aided by using the Reiki symbols. The lightning symbol (master level) seems particularly effective. With a psychic attack, it seems that Reiki can act like a shield that "deflects" the incoming energy. Once the attachment has been

broken, you can work to break it completely so that it doesn't reattach to the client after the session.
- Crystal wands or athames (Wiccan/witch tool) can help to cut any attachments or cords (energy fibres) from the client.
- You, and even the client, may need to speak out loud to the entity, making it clear that it's no longer welcome and that it needs to go back to wherever it came from.
- If you can't see, feel or sense the intrusion, or whatever it may be, ask the client how it feels now, what they are seeing, and what the entity, if there is one, is doing. They may be able to see or feel what is going on as you work, helping to direct you in your healing and clearing.
- After you have cleared what you can, Reiki the client, especially in the area where you have cut cords. These are the spirit fibres that an entity uses like a rope to cling to the person. Also Reiki the area that they felt the attack coming from. Make sure that they feel centred and balanced.

There can be a lot of work to do when someone feels that there is an esoteric issue. If you feel strong enough energetically to help someone this way, ensure that you protect yourself and trust your intuition. Do what feels right and listen to all of your senses, subtle body signs and emotional responses. Check in with your client and see how they are feeling.

Also make sure that you cleanse yourself after the session with a self-Reiki, and check in with yourself to ensure there is no energetic residue from the intrusion. Once again, do this by tuning in to all of your senses to notice if anything is off or out of balance with you. You can also use sage or other herbs or incense to cleanse yourself and your work space.

It may take several sessions to clear an unwanted attachment. We are very eager in our society to clear and complete things quickly, *now*, because we think that somehow this makes us better or more powerful as a healer (it doesn't). But if we look at the truth, rather than what we wish something to be, we may see that there is only so much we can do in one session. This is why it's really important to feel, with all of our senses, what is going on, rather than think our way through it.

It's so easy to declare that we have cleared an issue in one session. But what if we haven't? What if the client doesn't feel better afterwards? What if they can still feel the attachment or cords? Don't be tempted to hurry things along because you think that makes you a better healer. These things can take time, and it's better for the client if we are honest in our endeavours and our work.

A client once asked me to help her with a spirit that had attached itself to her. She was really upset and just wanted it to go. She explained to me that she was a psychic. This spirit wasn't hers but wanted her to pass a message on to someone that she knew. But she didn't want to; she just wanted it gone. I said I would try, so asked her to sit down. I put my hands on her shoulders and just went within, opening myself to Reiki. I don't see ghosts or spirits, but if I concentrate, I may become aware of a disturbance, or a different feel around the person in their aura or energy. I mentioned where I felt a disturbance around her, and she said that was where the spirit was hovering. I let Reiki flow, and after a few minutes or so, I started using a symbol in that area. I was also asking the spirit to go as it wasn't being helpful and couldn't be helped here. I asked the lady what was happening with the spirit, and she said it was moving away. Eventually it left her completely, and she thanked me with relief.

I had no idea what was happening because I couldn't see this spirit, but I acted instinctively, asking the client for guidance as I worked. At the end of it, the client was in a better place, relieved and feeling safe, and this is what matters.

We have no real language for these types of experiences in our society. So people don't know what to do or who to go to if they feel that something is wrong with their energy, with a part of themselves that we can't define. This is why healers encounter this type of issue, because it seems natural to people to come to us for this type of help.

I have occasionally helped people who have cord attachments – that is, energy holding on to a person that belongs to another, such as an old lover, a family member or a friend long gone. Cord attachments themselves aren't bad. When we engage in any type of relationship with another, we naturally create bonds, both emotional and energetic. Lovers have a bond and therefore cords, as do family members, friends, and so on. When a relationship goes bad, though, or we lose touch with a person, we may still hold those emotional attachments and therefore the energetic cords associated with that other person. This is why we can't easily release the past or let go of someone who is no good for us.

Cutting cords to sever these attachments, and therefore the emotional energy that they still hold, is relatively easy, but we must always make sure that we have the client's permission before cutting away each cord. There may be an emotional impact afterwards, and things that need talking through or dealing with. It could take several sessions to clear the emotional or energetic bonds completely, so we need to be in tune with what we feel and sense on the energy level as we work. I tend to use a crystal wand when cutting cords, but you don't have to – whatever works for you is fine. Always check with a client how they are feeling afterwards too, and then have a follow up with them within a week or so. Even if we do manage to clear the cords entirely, the emotional after-effects may last longer, so we need to look after our clients and their individual needs.

What if I have a spirit intrusion or come under a psychic attack?

Working purely with Reiki won't make you more susceptible to encountering a spirit entity or a psychic attack, but neither does it make you immune. You may simply come across such an event at some point in your life. Your connection with Reiki means that you are more likely to be aware when it does happen, and also be better equipped to deal with it, because you are able to understand what is happening so deal with it quickly and appropriately.

If you believe that you have a spirit intrusion or have come under a psychic attack, Reiki can help to clear it.

Visualise, sense or feel what it is that is unwanted within your energy presence. Get the feel and the shape of it:

- Tune into Reiki and perform hands-on healing, or Reiki meditation.
- Direct Reiki at the unwanted energy.
- Call on your guides, angels or deity to help remove the unwanted energies.
- Talk to it, telling it that it isn't welcome with you and that it needs to leave.
- Use the Reiki symbols, if you know them.
- Work intuitively, doing what feels right for you to do.
- Continue with Reiki for yourself even after the attachment has been released.
- Seek additional help from another healer, to help ensure that all of the unwanted and attached foreign energy is cleared.

You may need to do several regular sessions, at least once a day, to fully clear the energies. You may also need the help of another healer, as sometimes it can be easier for another person to do the work for us in these circumstances. Their extra help can shift the energies quicker and more completely. You could also use an energetic shield for yourself for the next week, to ensure the energies don't reattach to you, especially in the case of a psychic attack. Give yourself and also your home a full energetic cleansing, with sage or incense, and any other space that feels desirable to do so (such as your work space).

Even if you know where the psychic attack has originated from – who sent it to you – from a moral perspective I would never return ill intent. In this case there are two main options. You could cut the cords pertaining to that person, and then disassociate yourself from them as much as possible. If it's someone you can't remove entirely from your life, for example a work colleague, remain professional but distant, giving no emotional energy of your own towards them. A fire can't continue without fuel.

While every situation is different, and some may be more difficult or challenging than others, even if this person is goading you and wanting to get an emotional reaction from you, your distance and silence will act as a fire blanket, damping the fire that they are trying to feed. The other option is that you can send back through the energy attachment, or towards the other person, light and healing, the vibration of love. This, in energetic terms, has shown time and again to be the most effective method. It severely disrupts any bad energy coming in, weakening the intent of the person to send out bad energies to others, or, at its most potent, can even affect the person to the extent that their own energies change for the better. It also serves as a mode of forgiveness for ourselves so that we can release all frustration, fear and anger related to that person, therefore healing us from energetic wounds that may otherwise fester.

Some people say that if you believe in psychic attacks and spirit entities, this opens you up to them (so it's best not to believe in them). I don't see this as true. I think that when we believe in such phenomena, we simply become aware of when it happens around us or to us. It may be that some people who don't believe, or are unaware, are nevertheless affected by such energies.

If we don't remove unwanted energies, we can take on stuff that isn't our own, making us feel fatigued, drained, easily angered and perhaps behave in ways that isn't normal for us. It can make us feel weak and tired. In all cases, for ourselves and for others, Reiki can help us to remove and clear what isn't ours and what we don't want attached to us.

Summary

- Working with Reiki as its own modality doesn't open us up to spirit attachments or psychic attacks.
- These phenomena can happen in everyday life, but they are rare – always use your own intuition.
- Reiki can help to clear unwanted energies, for ourselves and others.
- Working with such phenomena isn't for everyone, and nor does it have to be.
- Work intuitively, and always for the highest good.

24. A Question Of Protection

"A man is but the product of his thoughts. What he thinks, he becomes."

- Gandhi

The idea of protection when practising Reiki is one that comes up a lot, both online and in classes. Some teachers teach this topic, and some don't. Everyone has their own ideas and opinions on this. So why does this concept of *protection* come up?

Well firstly, we are talking about energetic protection, not physical protection. We are talking about putting an energetic shield around ourselves prior to treating another, to protect our energy, and asking for the universe, Reiki and guides to protect us. The reason for this is so that we don't take on the energy of the client – or "negative energy", as some people say. We put a shield around ourselves to protect us from attachments or outside energy.

"Many practitioners and teachers feel the need to protect themselves from other people's negative energy. This need for protection comes from our own confused minds in which we think we are separate and not one with everything. Of course if we look deeply we are separate and yet also one with everything. Both happen simultaneously."

(Stiene, 2015)

Negative energy

Negative energy is a term used to describe something that we don't want around. Practitioners fear taking on "negative energy" from a client - but what do we really mean? It is a rather nebulous concept that never gets looked at closely.

What it really means is anger, fear and even old, stored emotions that are no longer helpful or needed in a person. *Bad* emotions. Except really, there are no bad emotions; there are only emotions that are misplaced. Emotions are like knives as tools: they are things to be used and hold no power in and of themselves. It's only the way in which we use the tool that determines whether it is *bad* or *good*.

In real terms, there is no such thing as negative energy. How can there be? When we think of what Reiki really is – universal *ki*, that is all around us, it simply is – how can it be negative? This idea of something as a negative force is simply an illusion that we, as human beings, carry around and interpret. Energy as the universal force that is within and without has no such distinction. Even if we take the idea of the Yin-Yang, the opposites entwined as a circle of black and white, there is no negative; simply opposing forces that work with each other – i.e. *balance*.

The perception of negative energy comes from a place of fear, and as soon as we label something in this way we place a sense of fear in our minds. What is there to fear? There is simply the universal life force that we tune into to help bring balance and well-being to a person's mind, body and spirit. When Reiki comes through us (not from us) and is connected with the recipient, how can it be possible that we as the practitioner can take anything on? Negative energy, positive energy, luck, fear, anxiety…? We do nothing. Reiki does everything.

So firstly we need to realise that there is nothing to take on; that negative energy is simply an illusion that we choose to interpret, to give a label to something nebulous, and that it doesn't exist when we really break it down and examine what we mean by it. From this, we can see that if there is no such thing as negative energy then there is no need to set protection, no need to put an energy shield around us.

Having said that, there is one reason that it may help to have a protective energy shield, which I explain further on in this chapter.

What most people mean when they say they are "taking on negative energy" is the *emotional feedback* from a person.

Emotional feedback

We have all experienced emotional feedback in our everyday life. We are not just verbal creatures – in fact, our verbal communication is the least of our interpersonal interactions. Visual cues and tone of voice tell us a lot more about what a person means and what they think, than what they actually say.

We know when someone is angry with us, without them saying a word. We know when we walk up to a group of people if there is an uncomfortable silence or if there has been an argument. Our instincts are highly tuned to social interactions because we depend on each other: as a species, we are social mammals. We are naturally tuned in to strong emotions, such as anger and fear, and the opposite is also true: happiness and joy are contagious!

As practitioners, dedicating ourselves to self-Reiki and meditation on a regular basis, working with *ki*, going inwards with focus, our instincts and inner awareness become heightened. This means that we are – or can be – more aware of non-verbal states, i.e. emotional feedback. We are likely to pick up on and understand when someone comes to us bubbling with anger, fear or anxiety, or even if we feel that someone just may not be a nice person. We pick up too when something seems to be off with someone. Maybe we clash with them, maybe we don't agree with their views, or maybe something just feels *wrong*. I think this is what healers sense when they term something as negative energy.

We know that we shouldn't make judgements, but we are human beings and snap judgements are going to run through our thoughts, even if we don't act on them. Sometimes we may come across someone who just doesn't feel comfortable to us, for whatever reason. We may then interpret this feeling as negative energy. Mostly, I think we pick up from the client on underlying emotions that we interpret as not useful and bad, such as anger, anxiety or fear. Unconsciously we may then have a fear that because we are connected with the client through Reiki, those emotions can leak through to us.

In traditional Reiki, the concept of emotional transference from the client to the healer isn't something that was considered as an occurrence. Indeed, if we are simply being Reiki, how can anything leak through? We are helping to bring balance and connection to our recipient, that is all. We are helping to align them with their own Reiki. If this is the case, then why do so many people think about – and fear – this taking on of emotions from another person? This is what I call empathy feedback. Maintaining a regular practice of remaining centred and grounded, and connecting with our own energy, can help us to balance, understand and maintain control of this sense of feedback – in other words, being strong in our foundations; having a strong base.

Empathy feedback

Practising meditation and Reiki can heighten our self-awareness and compassion. As we become more aware of self and our experiences, we also become more aware of others, including their emotional output. If this happens with a student of Reiki who is *already* naturally sensitive, who can pick up on others' emotions – an empath – then treating a person with a Reiki session is going to heighten that awareness even further.

What is happening isn't a *taking on* of negative energy, nor even of the recipient's emotions, but rather *picking up on* that person's feelings or underlying emotions. We may unconsciously pick up on old or recent trauma, heightened stress, underlying anger, and so on. We feel it, like a nebulous cloud around us, affecting us. *This doesn't mean that we have taken it into ourselves, just that we have become aware of it.* This strong ability of emotional empathy – or empathy feedback – can be both a blessing and a curse for a Reiki healer.

Empathy feedback can be a blessing because it can help us to understand where the pain is with that person, or what it is that needs healing. It can help us to understand what the person may be feeling. Empathy feedback includes both the emotional level and physical pains and sensations, such as the healer suddenly experiencing a headache or a sore throat. Physical or emotional feedback is useful, helping us to know how and where to focus Reiki. However, we should also be cautious here: once again, the ego trap can come into play. Sometimes a headache is just a headache of our own; a sore throat is the need to drink more water; and a strong emotion is our own from our daily life that we haven't cleared.

We must always take time to examine ourselves and ensure that we are not making easy and enthusiastic assumptions. Once we understand that what we are experiencing is empathy feedback from the client, we can work confidently, safe in the knowledge that Reiki will do its job for that person, without reflecting or leaking anything back to us. We can simply accept what we are feeling, knowing its source, and allow it to help guide us through the Reiki session. Feeling these things as a healer, whether it's physical or emotional feedback, doesn't mean that we have to take it into ourselves. It's just an experience. Think of it as a cloud around us – we become part of that cloud, but can allow it to move on of its own accord without breathing it in.

Empathy feedback can be a curse for some healers, however. If they experience these feelings, physical or emotional, very strongly, this can be overwhelming, uncomfortable and distracting. It can be too much for some natural empaths. Being aware of the cause of these feelings can be helpful, and knowing that we are not taking them on can also decrease the strength of feeling somewhat, but it's in this instance that I offer to my students the idea of protection.

I suggest using an energy shield for protection simply to help empaths who feel that they are taking on too much empathy feedback. Not to protect from negative energy, but to help themselves cope with any strong or overwhelming incoming feelings. In this instance, and in this way, an energy shield of protection can be a helpful tool. Once the empath feels more comfortable within themselves, and has practised Reiki for a while, they can choose to drop the use of protection, feeling more at ease with their practice. This isn't something that we have to keep doing forever; it's merely another tool on the path of developing our practice of Reiki. A protective shield can help us to feel secure and comfortable – and, yes, it does work! – but it can be left behind once we develop further in ourselves and along our own path.

If you haven't come across this idea of an energy shield and feel that it may be of use to you, it's a simple method, as outlined below:

- Sit with your eyes closed and take a few moments to come to a place of stillness within.
- Imagine or visualise a bubble surrounding you. A circle of light, encompassing you on all sides and above and below. It can be any colour (or none).
- Visualise the outer edges of this bubble, this shield, hardening like an eggshell.
- Say to yourself something like "I set this shield for protection, that nothing may get through except love and light."
- Spend a few moments in this visualisation.
- When you are done, there is no need to hold this – the shield will last as long as you need it to, for that day.

This may sound simple, but visualisation techniques are a key into our energy. What we can imagine or visualise intertwines with our energy. I have had students who have found this method effective and helpful.

Empaths can also struggle when they find themselves in busy places, such as towns and city centres. The energy of others can feel like a field of emotions pouring into the empath. Another technique that I use is to consciously draw my aura in close to my body. I focus on my aura, on the feel of it, and visualise bringing it in, so that all around it's only a few inches around my body. I repeat this several times until I notice a difference, which manifests as becoming more aware of myself and present in my own mind and body, rather than feeling scattered in my mind and slightly anxious. This focus on drawing in the aura can help to bring attention back to self and shut down the input of the emotional energy floating around us.

The other circumstance in which I would recommend using an energy shield is if you are working in a shamanic way – when you are doing more than just pure Reiki and are dealing with attachments, psychic attacks or spiritual intrusions. It's important when you are involved in such work to ensure that you look after your energy.

When we are wholly aware of ourselves and our understanding of Reiki and energy, we are more comfortable and confident in our work and our interactions with others. We can drop the fear, anxiety and labels, trusting in Reiki as energy that goes where it needs to, for the highest good.

Summary

- Some people suggest using protection to shield themselves from negative energy. But negative energy is a term used generally to describe strong emotions such as anger, fear and guilt – negative energy itself doesn't really exist.
- The practitioner of Reiki doesn't take on negative energy, or anything else from a client.

- Reiki practitioners and healers can experience emotional or empathy feedback, which can be strong emotions carried by the client.
- We can feel these emotions, and be aware of them, without taking them into ourselves – it's simply an awareness.
- Empaths, in particular, are more likely to feel strong physical sensations or emotions from the client.
- An energy shield can be a helpful tool for empaths who feel that they pick up on the client's emotions and find this too overwhelming. It can also be used to help in more-involved shamanic work.

Part V: Beyond personal practice

25. "Keep It Simple"

"Sometimes the questions are complicated and the answers are simple."

- *Dr Seuss*

I love the phrase "Keep It Simple". It's a life rule of mine.

Life can be overwhelming. It can be confusing. It can be too much. So what can we do when things start to get complicated? Keep It Simple!

Slow down; go back to the beginning; take the first step first; one thing at a time. "Keep It Simple" means all of these things. It reminds me to just pause, take a breath and think things through – go back to basics. This often helps me to clear my head and realise what needs to be done to move forward.

The same is true for Reiki. All you need is your intention and your intuition. Yes, it can feel like there is a lot to learn, it can become a deep practice, but at its heart it's also simple. Connect with universal *ki*, bring your mind into focus, hands on – Reiki. That is it. See what you feel and keep practising. This is Reiki stripped down to its core. Yet so many other practises have come into being around this – seeing colours, seeing auras, working with spirit attachments, being a psychic, and a whole host of other things too – that it can begin to feel complex and even overwhelming. It's absolutely fine if someone wishes to explore these elements, or indeed is a natural psychic, but the information — and therefore misinformation – out there can be confusing and distorting with regard to how Reiki intertwines and relates with these other practices.

Although Reiki does complement healing with crystals, angels, guides and/or energy attachments, *it isn't any of these things itself*. To be a student of Reiki, you don't have to add crystals or see angels. This isn't a requirement or an expectation. If you begin to wonder if you are "doing Reiki right" – Keep It Simple! If you begin to feel overwhelmed with information – Keep It Simple! Go back to basics: hands on, heal. Doing the very practice of Reiki will help to retain and maintain your inner balance – calm mind, calm body! This is the very essence of Reiki.

No matter how many years' experience a person has, no matter which level we are at or how many years we have been a practitioner or a master, we should all be engaging regularly with self-Reiki. This is because we need to maintain our inner calm and well-being, and that only comes with continual dedication and practice. We are always changing, and our lives are constantly changing. We are creatures with emotions and thoughts and feelings, and so there are many layers of us to be unpacked, examined, recover from and healed. There will be many situations that will make us feel anger, disappointment, fear and anxiety. We keep doing the hands-on self-Reiki to reap the benefit of clearing us out from within, which can help us to see calmly and clearly and to know ourselves better, and to then be able to help others with Reiki. How can we help others if we haven't been doing self-Reiki? How can we help others to achieve balance and calm if we ourselves are not? Always go back to basics. Go back to "just Reiki", to self-healing.

The practice of *Gassho* is a really good example of keeping it simple: *Gassho* is the *hands together in prayer position*, which we do in Reiki before self-treatment and treating others. It is that space where we connect within, connect with Reiki, letting all outside distractions go. We can use *Gassho* as a meditation. Sitting, with our hands in prayer position, and focusing on the feel of those hands touching each other. Focusing on breathing. That is all. Just this. Every time the mind wanders off, gently bring it back to the focus on the hands, on breathing. Focus on this for 10, 15, 20 or 30 minutes. Do this meditation every day for at least a week, and you will see what I mean. It really is the ultimate "Keep It Simple".

Trusting your intuition

With each session being different and dependent upon the client's requirements as well as our own comfortable way of working, our intuition can play an important role in how to conduct each session. Does it feel right to get the crystals out? Does it feel like I should call on angels? Do I start at the head, as usual, or come to the middle (or the feet) first? Trusting our intuition can have a positive impact on the healing process. When or if things seem overwhelming because of all the information we have absorbed - Keep It Simple! Trusting our own intuition can be helpful in bringing us back to what is right for this moment.

We may have heard other Reiki healers talking about what they pick up or see from clients, and what they can tell them about their issues, and this may make us feel somewhat less if we don't or can't do the same. But every session is what it is within that space and time. We can only act for our recipient's best interests when we are comfortable with ourselves and trust ourselves. We don't always need to see or sense things – just to act within that Reiki space, letting the experience flow naturally.

Sometimes during a session, we may feel or "see" things in relation to a client; we may intuit certain life experiences of theirs, or what is going on for them at an energetic or spiritual level. Some people label this as a psychic experience, but I have never thought of myself as psychic. I think of it in this way: when we see things in our mind about a client that they haven't told us, something that comes through in thought or vision during a session, it's the empathy link through the oneness of Reiki – like floating down the same river (the energy stream of Reiki) and seeing the same things along that river. We see a reflection in the energy stream as we are with that client.

In this case, we would do well to exercise caution. Is our ego getting in the way? Are we jumping to conclusions, our imagination presenting certain assumptions about our client to us, rather than it really being something outside of ourselves that we have picked up? This is where we need to know ourselves deeply, to understand the difference between imagination and intuition at work. Our intuition is a strong ability that increases naturally as we engage with Reiki, but it can take time for us to trust it, and to trust ourselves.

It can be easy to underestimate the impact of a simple, pure Reiki session – just Reiki – with hands on or just off the body, allowing the essence to flow, moving to each position where we want or need to go. The simplicity of Reiki is a wonderful and sometimes deep experience. It can even be profound – sometimes, not always! Even a session that the recipient only says felt "relaxing" can have enormous benefits.

How many times do you hear from family, friends and colleagues "I find it hard to relax" or "I'm working too hard, but I have so much to do!" Relaxation is a gift indeed. Sometimes it can take a few days or even weeks for a person to realise and understand just what effect the Reiki session had for them. Don't be in a rush for an answer or to see the benefit … it will happen. A simple Reiki session is just as effective and beautiful as a session with additions. The majority of my sessions with clients are just simple Reiki, with no extras and no psychic experiences.

Our job as a healer is simply to connect with Reiki and to be available for the client, allowing them to experience whatever they need. Yes, we may wish to include crystals, or we may be a psychic, or we may want to work with angels. But our job isn't to fix people, or tell them about their past or their future, or to include every possible alternative or esoteric methodology. Our job is simple: allow Reiki to flow. This goes for our own self-healing too; just be with Reiki.

Whatever you are doing with Reiki, however you work, whatever you include, just remember: "Keep It Simple!"

Summary

- Reiki is a simple practice – hands on, connect with Reiki, let it flow.
- Many different beliefs have become entwined with Reiki, but are not part of Reiki.
- There are many other modalities we can add to our healing basket, choosing what feels right for us.
- Our job as a Reiki practitioner or healer is simply to connect with Reiki and to attend to our client's needs.
- Trust your intuition, which strengthens through regular Reiki practice, time and patience.
- Don't be persuaded or sidetracked by the ego-mind.
- Always remember: "Keep It Simple".

26. You Don't Have To Be Perfect!

"If you want others to be happy, practice compassion. If you want to be happy, practice compassion."

- Dalai Lama XIV, The Art of Happiness

Somewhere along the line, we have created a sense that those who work with certain practices should be virtually perfect. Today there seems to be an implication of "I'm more spiritual than thou" that has become a competitive undercurrent. I want to address this and lay the idea of "You have to be perfect or almost perfect to be spiritual" to rest.

When we enter the world of healing and spirituality or spiritual teachings, the imagery that comes to mind is that of compassion, healing the self and self-awareness. All of this promotes an image of someone in control, knowledgeable and spiritual. What does *spiritual* actually mean? This depends on who you ask: the term and concept of "spiritual" isn't actually defined in our minds but is, like the word *healing*, subjective. It can mean different things to different people. It does *not* mean "religious". Of course, religion can incorporate spirituality, and many people would say that through their religious beliefs they are spiritual. Spirituality is separate from religion, though, and we as individuals can be spiritual without being religious.

Spiritual means to have a sense of inner self beyond our physical being, and a connection to something greater or outside of our self. This sense can include God(s), Goddess(es), conscious universe and divine. It doesn't even have to be defined: some people believe that there is a "greater power" out there, helping or influencing us, without giving this power a label or name. For others, being spiritual means working on and paying attention to the inner self – our spirit, if you will – to become more intuitive, self-aware and connected to nature and humanity. It can be about our own moral compass and following what feels right within, finding guidance and answers from a variety of religious or spiritual paths.

Reiki healers, masters and teachers are probably super-spiritual, and they have all the answers. Their life is pretty much perfect and they never get ill. They don't have any quirks or foibles – if they do, they aren't genuine, right? I really wish that I could say this is true!

Why should we be perfect? Are we teachers and practitioners of Reiki not human beings too? We are allowed to smoke, drink, eat meat, be too fat or too thin, get stressed, have problems in our lives and *still be seeking answers*.

People who attend Reiki training workshops often describe themselves as spiritual, but not everyone does, and nor do you have to. We can be a decent, kind and compassionate human being without being spiritual. Yes, I would describe Reiki as a spiritual practice ... when we get to the deep understanding of what it can do for us and open up within us. When we practice self-Reiki regularly, when we understand the concepts of the precepts and the symbols and the deep healing, then it's spiritual. But we don't have to be spiritual to practise Reiki, nor do we need to be perfect: in fact, we may well be a bit of a mess. This is the point of doing Reiki, after all – to help ourselves find the answers and to become a better person.

Whatever we believe, whatever we think, whatever we go through in our life, we get exactly what it is that we need from Reiki. Each of us practises in our own way, and we shouldn't judge others because their way may differ from ours. We are all on our own journey, and being aware of how Reiki is helping us in our own life, with our own healing, is what truly matters.

The point of practising Reiki isn't that we *are perfect*, but that we are seeking to become better in ourselves and more in line with our inner being, our authentic self, all the time. This is true for practitioners and teachers as well. The idea of a "perfect person" is a fallacy. We are all perfect in our very human imperfections!

Yes, of course, as a practitioner or teacher we should know our subject thoroughly; yes, we should have self-awareness; and yes, we should recognise our own issues and emotional disturbances and be more calm and in control. But that doesn't equate to perfection. We seek to improve ourselves through Reiki because we recognise its beauty and benefits for our mind, body and spirit. We may still be seeking answers and figuring things out in our own lives, but that doesn't mean we can't teach Reiki or be a practitioner. Some people seem to have this idea that a "true" Reiki student, healer, professional practitioner or teacher should not:

- eat meat
- smoke
- drink alcohol

But that they should regularly engage in yoga, qi gong, tai chi etc.

While all of the above is noble and can certainly help on a spiritual or holistic healing path, and is perhaps good for us mentally and physically, *it isn't a requirement* of a Reiki healer or teacher. If it's your choice to follow the above, that is of course absolutely great. But why should we judge people because they indulge in the odd glass of wine? Or smoke? Or eat meat? Does this affect our capacity to *be* Reiki? It certainly doesn't stop the flow of the energy – the connection. It doesn't affect a person's empathic or natural ability to connect with others and help them to feel at ease. Would we deny a natural healer because they eat meat?

If we choose to go with a healer or teacher who fits into our own spiritual ideals, such as a vegan, non-smoking, tee-total yoga-practising teacher, that is well and good. But we do not *have* to be so perfect to be a practitioner or teacher. Don't feel guilty if you smoke or drink alcohol – hey, you are human, and your teacher is human too. We are all on our own journey, and I hope that we can appreciate each others' too.

Some healers have gone through a lot of trauma in their lives. It's healing through this difficult and painful time that brings them to working with Reiki. People who have faced trauma can still be experiencing pain, emotionally or physically, but, because of their own experiences, they can be amazing healers – they understand how to connect with others and to empathise with them. They are aware of the needs of a person who comes for healing, and how to talk to them. We will discuss trauma and healing in the next chapter.

Summary

- Reiki healers and teachers aren't perfect!
- We are human beings, and we are allowed to have our foibles and choices in life.
- We are all seeking our own ways, and we are all on our own life journey.
- Don't ever let someone tell you that you can't practise Reiki because you eat meat, smoke, drink, don't do yoga or aren't looking after your body.
- We should all be seeking to become better in ourselves, but this is an ongoing, lifetime search!
- Your own life experiences can help you connect with your clients or recipients.

- Those who have been through some form of trauma in their lives can come to Reiki as part of their healing process and can make excellent healers.

27. A Healer Has To Have Come Through Trauma To Be A Good Healer (And Why This Isn't True)

"Sukha is the state of lasting well-being that manifests itself when we have freed ourselves of mental blindness and afflictive emotions... It is the joy of moving toward inner freedom and the loving kindness that radiates towards others."

- *Matthieu Ricard, 'Happiness'*

"A *real* healer has to have gone through trauma to be any good" is a phrase that I have often heard repeated.

A person who has trials to overcome, who is going through a huge healing process, or who has experienced any kind of trauma, is often drawn to Reiki. Many people have their own story to tell of trials and tribulations, and they recognise Reiki as a gentle and effective self-directed healing method. It's a wonderful treatment to help in the ongoing journey of recovery and healing, whichever stage we are at: still healing; recovered but with the metaphorical scars still new and raw; or helping to let go of a past that is long gone, yet still holds us in its ghostly chains. Reiki has been a helpful path for many people.

Those who seek to heal from their wounds, to find ways to help themselves and continue their ongoing healing, can and do make wonderful Reiki healers. This is because they have often travelled a path of self-examination and self-awareness and understand what it means to have been through darkness and to face the challenge of coming through it. Reiki healers who have been through their own trauma can naturally empathise with others who are having or have been through a difficult and challenging time. They can connect with others, and critically also know how to speak to them. They know when not to say too much, when to back off and be gentle. They know the right words for encouragement. It's the counselling – the discussion and natural support – as well as the reassurance they bring in the direct treatment that can be effective in helping others.

This can be a delicate line to walk. A practitioner doesn't have to be perfectly healed from their own experience to be able to be effective, just healed enough. Indeed, some people say that you are never fully healed: just like grief, trauma isn't something you get over but is something that you learn to live with – it shapes a part of your life but no longer controls your life. Yet, if a healer is still affected by their experiences, and they are not healed "enough", this can impact on their own emotional state and their interactions with others. Their own inner turbulence can get in the way of being able to help and heal others. Each of us must make our own judgements about whether we feel we are ready to help others, or still need to work on ourselves.

Because Reiki is a gentle treatment and doesn't require us to talk about our issues, what we have been through or how we feel, it's an excellent therapy to help those recovering from trauma. It can work wonderfully alongside counselling, for example, acting as a counter to all of the talking and self-examination, allowing the person to just lay down and relax, letting Reiki flow through them to bring some balance and peace. It may help to aid the recovery process, and for someone to begin to release feelings of fear, anxiety, guilt or shame.

Reiki isn't a quick fix. It won't heal the trauma immediately, but it can certainly help that healing process. It can bring self-forgiveness, forgiveness or a release of anger; it can bring someone into the present, rather than living in the past. It can help someone realise who they are beyond their trauma – who they really are at their inner core.

All of us have had our own troubles, trials and challenges. We may have taken a few knocks in life, even if we haven't experienced a serious trauma of any kind, whether physical or mental. Something that may seem like a small thing to someone else may, in fact, have had a significant impact on our life. None of us are completely unscarred, though our scars will be different shapes, colours and sizes. We all have something to bring in helping others with Reiki. We all have a way that we can connect with others: none of us are a blank slate, with no experiences. Whatever we have gone through, and how we have dealt with it or are dealing with it, can be something that another person connects with.

If we are lucky enough to have pretty much coasted through life, and feel that we haven't really had any bad experiences, does this mean that we have nothing to offer? Does this mean we can't be an effective healer? Do we think that Reiki energy, the consciousness, the divine will, or oneness, makes that distinction? No, of course not. Only our own feelings about ourselves – or the assumptions or expectations that others have of us – affect our ability to help others with Reiki.

While those who have been through trauma or a serious healing experience can make excellent, empathic and understanding healers, we don't have to have been through an awful or tragic experience to understand Reiki or to be able to help others. Self-healing helps us to grow an awareness of ourselves at a deeper level; to recognise and start to manage our emotional ups and downs, and our behavioural reactions to and with others, as well as our own habits and defences. Self-healing helps to open our compassion and respect for all people and beings. Reiki doesn't care about our experiences, our personal journey. The energy flows freely and indiscriminately for all people, from every background. Therefore, *of course* you can be an effective healer for others, even if you haven't been through a traumatic experience.

A Question of Reiki

You might think, *But what do I have to offer others?* The "soft skills", as they are often termed, are part and parcel of helping others. Your unique character, your youness is what people will react to and find a connection with. Are you a good listener? Kind-hearted? Generous? Naturally empathic? (You don't have to have gone through the same experience as someone else to be able to empathise with them.) Are you no-nonsense and able to get to the heart of a matter? Are you a parent who understands the challenges of raising children? Have you been through heartache, or grief? Never underestimate the value of your own life experiences.

It isn't just our emotional connection with others that can help when we give a treatment, but the skills that we have picked up through our own life experiences can become of great value. When I set up my Reiki business, my job background of customer service and contact centre work seemed a million miles from the world of energy healing. Yet to keep a business going, those very skills served me incredibly well: administration, organisation of my paperwork, schedules, appointments and timekeeping were necessary background skills to keep it all ticking over smoothly. The customer service aspect came into play in being able to speak to people on the phone prior to a session, as well as at the session itself. Listening and sounding professional as well as being personable.

I tried *so* hard to begin with, worrying what other people would think about me and how I came across. I was so nervous! Then I realised something: I didn't need to *try*. I just needed to *be*. To be me! That was when I felt more comfortable and at ease, and I really do think that came across. To be honest, to understand that we don't always have all the answers, that I may not be able to help every situation – but what I *can* be, what I can *do*, is Reiki. Allow Reiki to speak for itself – fall into the flow of Reiki, and be your very own authentic self.

That is all we need to be a successful and natural healer. We can be a fantastic healer if we have been through trauma and are healing, and we can be a fantastic healer if we have not been through trauma. Whatever our background, experiences or challenges ... each one of us has the capacity to *Be Reiki*.

Summary

- You don't have to have been through a traumatic experience in your life to be a good Reiki healer. But neither do you *not* have to have been through trauma to be a good Reiki healer.
- Our experiences, whether challenging, difficult or traumatic, can help us to empathise, understand and connect with others.
- Whatever your background, you have something to bring to the experience of helping others through Reiki.
- Our practice and dedication to and with Reiki opens our understanding, and therefore our own self-awareness, to heal at a deeper level.
- Just be you!

28. A Little Bit Of Business

"When we give cheerfully and accept gratefully, everyone is blessed."

- Maya Angelou

Throughout this book, I have referred to a person receiving a Reiki treatment as *your recipient* or *client*. I have used these terms interchangeably, to mean simply *the person that you are giving a treatment to*. If you don't currently practise Reiki on a professional basis, you may be considering whether this is something that you would like to do in the future. Level two in most Reiki branches, certainly in Usui and Jikiden, is the "professional practice" level and enables you to go into business.

Master training is for those who wish to teach Reiki. Within level two, training should include what you need to know to go into professional service, although not every teacher covers this topic: the Reiki curriculum isn't regulated, and teachers can teach in whichever way suits them. There are certain topics that really should be covered at each level, such as the history of Reiki at level one, along with the direction for self-healing and healing others, and at level two the symbols and their meanings, and distant Reiki.

Professional practice as a subject seems to be considered as optional. However, it's quite difficult to set up your own business if you have no experience or knowledge of it, as I found out myself when I took the leap of faith and started my own business back in 2013. I learnt the hard way, and I spent months finding out what I needed to know to make the business work. Because of that, I pass on the relevant information to my students at level two, hoping to make things a little easier for them. I still see this come up quite a bit on social media, with people asking questions around starting a business:

- Do I need insurance?
- Do I need waivers (consent forms)?
- Do I need to join a Reiki association/body?
- Do I need a website?
- How do I get clients?

I don't intend to go into the fine details here, but I hope that a little information will help you if you ever decide that you, too, would like to start taking on paying clients.

There is a lot of discussion around online Reiki classes and whether these are as good as in-person classes. I am not talking about independent teachers who teach live video classes, but about the courses that are offered by big companies. I have never taken an online class, so I can't say how good they are. However, Reiki associations and most insurance companies don't recognise online classes and the distant attunement that they offer for students. Insurance requires the attunement to be in person with your teacher, as this is the only way it can be verified that the attunement definitely took place. Therefore, if you want to set up professional practice, in the UK at least, in-person attunements are required.

I think online courses are good options for people who can't get to an in-person class for any reason, or for those who feel they may struggle in a full-day class because of mental or physical issues. I think that there is a place for them in today's world, but I am wary of them becoming the norm,

A Question of Reiki

because I don't believe that they can offer the same support for the student as an in-person class, where the teacher is on hand, can explain things at your pace, can answer whatever questions come up, and can support the student.

Some people have profound reactions to learning Reiki, either through the teachings or with the attunement, and the master is immediately on hand to guide, talk and support them. A good teacher notices when reactions are occurring, as the student themselves may not be able to express how they are feeling. A teacher can pick up on this and talk about why certain reactions may be happening, or have a one-to-one conversation with that person. You also know how much time and effort a teacher has spent in putting together the materials and the class, tailoring the class as needed.

As well as this, an in-person class offers the benefit of sharing and learning with other students. I have found that this works really well, as people share their thoughts and own knowledge and understanding of various topics – in other words, students learn not only from the teacher, but from each other too. Then you also have the practical hands-on healing that students get to do with each other, having the opportunity to give each other a Reiki treatment to build their confidence and understanding during the class.

A student in a level two class once asked me, "Heidi, what do you get out of teaching us this? You're basically creating competition for yourself, certifying us as being able to start our own Reiki business!"

Well, yes, she was right to a certain extent, but this isn't how I think about it. The obvious and straightforward answer to this question is, "Well, you are paying me to take this course, so the first thing I get out of it is a financial reward!" This is true, but it isn't the reason for teaching Reiki. It's hard work holding classes, and most teachers spend a lot of time at home organising and preparing for each course. We are also dealing with members of the public, and short-notice cancellations and challenging people are not unknown. Holding classes isn't, by any means, an easy life, and you never know how many people are going to book onto a class. One time it may be full, the next time it may be a handful of people, so the level of income isn't guaranteed.

As for the point about "creating competition", this isn't how I view Reiki. Of course we all want clients to come to us, and our ego may get antsy when we hear of another practitioner nearby, but Reiki benefits all of us. Though many people now know about this modality, it still isn't a mainstream practice. The more of us that are out there *being* Reiki, sharing Reiki and setting up a Reiki practice, the more it will come to be seen as something normal rather than "that weird thing a friend of mine is into!"

Let us look at it another way. In your local town, how many restaurants are there? And coffee shops? And hairdressers? Any locality thrives on variety, giving something for everyone. What if there was only one restaurant and you didn't like the menu? What if there was only one hairdresser and you didn't like the way they cut your hair? Similarly, each of us as a Reiki practitioner has something unique to offer, and our particular flavour isn't going to be for everyone.

What if the Reiki practitioner down the road from me knows how to deal with addictions, but I am not comfortable in that area? What if I am good at dealing with depression and anxiety, but that other Reiki practitioner likes to bring through angels and ascended masters? You see, we need what each of us can bring. It's wonderful to build up a local support network and friendly community of Reiki practitioners, other healers and complementary therapists, to go to when we ourselves may need advice or a healing. I have made a lot of friends through local mind, body and spirit exhibitions, as well as speaking to people online in specialist Reiki groups. We don't need to view our business as competition – remember, no labels, no attachments, no judgements.

The other point is that I absolutely love teaching Reiki! It doesn't feel like work; it feels like happiness! I love meeting people and hearing their personal stories, and seeing what Reiki begins to mean for them and how it can benefit them in their everyday life. And I really love the "ripple effect" that it creates. How many of those students go out there and start helping out friends, who then want to know more – and perhaps these friends also look up a Reiki class? How many lives are changed, in a small way or a profound one, because of Reiki? Rippling out, and I am just one small link in an ever-growing chain.

Reiki, at any level right up to master, is for our personal and spiritual development first and foremost, although traditionally one was expected to teach if they were to undertake the master level as that is what it was for: to pass on the teachings. Yet in our society today, many people benefit from the master-teacher training even for personal reasons, as it fills in and fulfils our understanding of Reiki. Many students find that it feels like a completion of their training and their own spiritual development. It also means that you can pass on your knowledge, and perform the *Reiju*, on an informal basis – i.e. for a friend or family member, even if you don't want to hold full classes.

So, what should you do if you are thinking about taking that step into professional practice? The first thing I will say, and that doesn't seem to get spoken about much online, is that Reiki practice *is not a money maker!* You are unlikely to earn a fortune doing this ... unless you become an internationally renowned teacher in great demand. You may struggle even to make a full-time earning out of it, so have a plan before you begin. You may want to consider having another form of income to rely on, so perhaps start off your Reiki business part-time, just a day or two a week, until you have a strong and regular client base. You are going to need to put a lot of work in before you start, researching what you need to know and thinking about what works for your business.

I see on social media some answers to the question of starting a business as: "Visualise being successful ... follow the Law of Attraction ... bring good energy to you by knowing that you will succeed..."

That is fine as far as it goes, and there is certainly no harm in positive intention and visualisation, but that on its own isn't going to guarantee you success. You need to put the work in and to know what to do to create and maintain your business - just as Mikao Usui told us to "work hard," in one of the precepts.

The problem with people asking questions in social media groups about starting a business is that a lot of these groups are global, and naturally the rules of business practice vary from country to country. You need to find out the rules and regulations for the country you are in.

In the UK, you need insurance, and you can join, but are not *required* to, an associative Reiki body such as The Reiki Association, The UK Reiki Federation or The Reiki Guild. Each country has its own rules, and in the US those rules vary from state to state. You can always look up a local Reiki association and ask them what you need to set up practice.

You need to know your country's regulations on self-employment: tax, accounting, advertising and confidentiality, to name a few. To start your own business, you are most likely going to be self-employed, so you will be doing all of your accounts, your advertising, your paperwork, your client contact, your record-keeping and your social media posting. A lot of work goes on behind the scenes to keep a business running smoothly. While Reiki is a fantastic business to be in, it isn't all seeing a client and sprinkling magic over them and feeling good. It is a business and has to be treated as such to work for you and to be financially viable.

How are you going to get your name out there? How are you going to let your local community know that you are up and running and a good person to see to help them deal with their physical, mental and emotional stresses and challenges? Don't just create a Facebook or Instagram page, or a website, and then sit back and think that the work is done! That only gets you so far. You may want to think about flyers and leaflets and posters, and where you can hand these out locally. Do you want to do talks for charities or local businesses? Offer discounts to a section of the population, e.g.

students, low-income households or nursing staff? Do you want to specialise in your treatments: helping pregnant women or trauma-related issues, for example? I have found that word of mouth is still one of the best ways to get business, and building a reputation is great, but it does take time.

Be patient, put in the hard work, have a plan, get going, talk to people, get your friends to talk to people, and allow it to take its course. Getting clients will happen, but not overnight.

Do you need a website? That is up to you. The advantage that a website has over just a social media page is that you build your content on a website, put in all of the information that you want on it, and it's there, all done. People Google your name or "Reiki", or whatever is relevant, and they will see from your website everything they need to know. Social media on the other hand is a machine that needs constant feeding: you need to be continually updating new posts and content to get seen, and that can become tiring, draining and exhausting (unless you are someone who loves social media, and you are good at it!) There are plenty of website platforms that allow you to just add the content you want, without having to do too much of the technical stuff, so it's worth having a little look around and again, researching before you do anything to find what is right for you.

Then you need to think about *where* – will your practice be based in an established clinic, or from your home, or will you buy or rent your own premises? Each of these has advantages and disadvantages. If you are going to set aside a room at home to work from, you need to find out if your insurance will cover that, and let your home insurance know. Are you comfortable with strangers coming into your home? If not, working from a clinic is a good option, but more expensive as you will be paying them to rent a room. Obviously buying or renting your own premises is an expensive option, but if you have the money, you will need to look into all of the regulations that come with this option.

Social media can be a wonderful place for help and support, but don't rely on it to have all the answers that you need: this is going to be *your* business, *your* way, in *your* hometown. Put in the research and the work and the planning. I would recommend that before you leap into professional practice, you spend a good amount of time working on your self-Reiki and Reiki for willing family and friends. This will give you a good grounding in the different ways that a session can go, the feel of the energy, the outcomes, and just as importantly, the discussions and questions that arise. When you feel that you are ready, make sure you are comfortable talking to complete strangers about Reiki, about what they may experience, what effects it may have, and about answering any questions. You never know who is going to be walking through your door.

29. And Finally…

"How do I know where creation comes from?
I look inside myself and see it."

- *Tao Te Ching*

Reiki is such a beautiful practice and system to work with because of its simplicity. It requires nothing from us but to go with the flow and to *just be*. We don't even need to know what it is within ourselves or others that needs healing for that healing to occur. We don't need to delve or dwell on the issues if we don't want to: Reiki does, Reiki is, Reiki moves through us and creates balance and harmony within.

Yet it's also rich and complex under the surface, as I hope this book has served to illustrate. We can keep going deeper, into our own self and into Reiki, and into all the other strands that it complements and intertwines with, whether that is on the medical side, with complementary therapies, or the esoteric aspects. There are so many ways that we can go, so many paths we can travel, to learn more.

Reiki has grown new branches from its original roots. We have Jikiden Reiki that stayed in Japan, and then we have the Usui Reiki that Mrs Takata brought to us in the West, and the various newer strands that grew afterwards. Each of these has their own practices, their own symbols, but

And Finally...

at the heart it's all energy – or *essence* – based healing. It's all universal or spiritual healing, for the benefit of body, mind and spirit. It's up to each of us to discover and explore what is right for us, at this time. We can stick to one practice, or train in several modalities.

We can choose whether to incorporate angels, ascended masters, spirit guides, and so on – if this feels right for us personally. We can add our own psychic gifts with Reiki, or not. We can work with crystals, or not. We can be a massage therapist and a Reiki practitioner, or a reflexologist or aromatherapist, or a counsellor or hypnotherapist. All these therapies blend well with the simplicity of Reiki. Or we can just be Reiki!

There is no right or wrong in how we choose to practise Reiki for ourselves and for others. Just because someone else says something – face to face, on social media, or in a book – does it feel true to you? Does it sit right for you? Does it work for you? Try things out. Experiment. Trust your intuition. If something works – great, keep doing it. If it doesn't work – leave it by the wayside. My own Reiki practice, in my personal development, professional practice and teaching, has gone through so many alterations as I change my view, perspective and understanding. I am in a very different place now to where I was five years ago, and I was in a different place five years ago to where I was five years before that. There's no point in doing something or believing something if it's coming from a place of prescription and not from your heart. Take on board all of the information that you absorb, and the advice that others give, but trust yourself just as much (if not more).

Almost everything in Reiki is a tool, to help us to understand at a deeper level and to develop further: the symbols are a tool, a road-map to enhance our understanding; the chakra system is a tool to help us gain some insight. These are useful, but we don't need to get hung up on them. None of these tools make us a better healer, more effective or more powerful. We choose to use the tools that help us to develop and enhance our own understanding. And no one branch of Reiki is better or more powerful than another.

Working with angels, guides or spirit beings is one way of connecting and understanding all that is around us – again, you are not somehow less if you don't connect with such non-physical beings. Some people naturally see and feel them, while some people want to and work at it, and that's great. Other don't, and that is great too. Reiki isn't going to judge you. And don't forget that when you work with a client or recipient they also come in all shapes and sizes of beliefs – some people will be quite relieved that you don't start talking about the "woo woo" stuff. Some people just want to lie down, relax and feel better. They just want the experience of Reiki. Others will adore feeling the presence of angels, or knowing they have their own spirit guide. We are all different, and we should acknowledge and celebrate that. Travel your own path, in your own time, your own way. There is no rush or end goal here … Enjoy the journey!

I could talk for days about Reiki, I could use 10,000 words to describe it (or a book…), and I still won't describe it in an accurate, definitive way. What and how we feel about Reiki is subjective, which is why there are many books out there, many descriptions and many opinions. After everything, after all of the words, techniques, diagrams, and more – I think we need to accept that Reiki is both simple and complex, and that there is no getting away from the fact that it is, at least in part, a mystical or inexplicable practice that needs to be experienced to be truly understood. It's a mystery, and I love that about it. So do the practices. Do the self-healing (if you have taken a course in Reiki); go to a Reiki practitioner and have a healing from another person; use the tools within the system; explore the meditations, and sitting with nature, and anything else that you like, and remember:

And Finally…

There are no shortcuts
Time, patience, and practice, practice, practice!

I would like to leave with you some final thoughts about Reiki.

How do we define Reiki? How do we explain Reiki to others who haven't heard of it, or who have heard of it but know very little about it? New students of Reiki (and also wiser, older students) struggle to answer the question, "Okay, you do Reiki … but what *is* it?"

As a new student of Reiki, I had difficulty answering this. The very simple explanation that I gave was, "It's healing energy!" Nice, simple, perfectly explained. But is it? What does this actually mean? What would that answer mean to people who have no experience of holistic healing or of spiritual energy? Is it *really* an answer? As I became more familiar with Reiki, and the practice, I started thinking a bit more about this question:

"Reiki is a like a moving meditation that opens our awareness and our connection to oneness, to allow us to heal from the inside out."

As I progressed further, I started thinking a little bit more about this. Now when I teach, I still use the term "energy / spiritual energy", but I know that it's so much more than this. Reiki just *is*. Having the experiences by doing the practices helps us to comprehend the depth of Reiki. To really understand its meaning, we need to surrender. Surrender what? Just that: just surrender.

How do we define Reiki? How do we describe it as more than just energy or essence? I put this question to my Reiki student and friends' circle. Interestingly, each person gave a different answer:

- "Universal love"
- "Compassion"
- "Spiritual energy"
- "A set of tools and practices to help us open our awareness and go deeper, which enables healing"

I don't think that any of these, on their own, accurately defines Reiki. Describes, yes; defines, no. But I do think that Reiki is all of these things together: just as a car is not its steering wheel, or its engine, or its seats, or its wheels – yet it is all of these things together.

"The sum is greater than its parst", as the saying goes.

That last description given of Reiki, that it is a set of tools and practices to help open up our awareness, was an interesting one, and definitely I would agree, with a caveat: if this is the case, then how is it that new students at the first level of Reiki, who have only just had the attunement, are able to access Reiki and heal themselves as well as others?

How is a student who doesn't consider themselves "spiritual" able to access Reiki? How are we able to do it for others, who haven't themselves had training yet can feel the Reiki? You see the problem that we run into when we start really thinking about what is Reiki? A person going for a healing from another person needs to know nothing about Reiki, yet receives the benefit of it. Is Reiki spiritual? Is it love? Is it compassion? Is it meditation? I think it engenders all of these things, and certainly it can help us to open our own awareness and develop our inner self, but new students don't need to feel all this to access Reiki, nor a person who comes for a session.

Reiki is Reiki. Describe it in the way that feels right to you. My purpose with this is not to proscribe a meaning of Reiki to you, but to leave you, perhaps, with deeper or alternative thoughts to how you think of or understand this universal force of *ki* that we engage with for holistic healing and well-being. We don't need to get hung up on descriptions and definitions; we don't need to feel that we are right (and "they" are wrong); all that matters is the experience … just the experience.

"What is Reiki?"

"I really don't know … A laying of hands to help us to feel better from the inside out, to help physically, mentally and emotionally, a bit like

And Finally…

meditation that someone does for and with you. A way to heal into wholeness. Want to give it a try?"

Go on. Go and just Reiki!
Have fun with your practice. Enjoy.
Reiki blessings to you, wherever your journey takes you.

> **"Reiki is love,**
> **Love is wholeness,**
> **Wholeness is balance,**
> **Balance is well-being,**
> **well-being is freedom from disease."**

- *Attributed to Mikao Usui.*

Appendix

Glossary of Terms

Angels – Non-physical beings available to help humans, full of goodness, love and protection. Angels may appear as humans or light, or just as an indefinable but felt presence. "Angel" comes from the Greek word *Angelos*, meaning "messenger". The concept of angels or angel-like beings are found in many different cultures.

Attunement – *see Reiju*

Boddhisatva – A being that has attained enlightenment, and vows or chooses to help others to also achieve enlightenment. A being of ultimate compassion. In Buddhism the idea of a "Boddhisatva" is quite a strict list, and examples of Boddhisatvas are Buddha and Kwan Yin.

Chakras – *lit.* "vortex", *or* "wheel". The word and the concept originate from India and refers to energetic vortices in the body's energy system that align with our emotional, mental and spiritual states. Chakra centres can become unaligned and therefore need help and work to become balanced and aligned to keep us holistically healthy.

Chi/Ki/Qi – The subtle energy that is in every living thing. We can call this spiritual energy which is manipulated through practices such as tai chi and qi gong. *chi* and *qi* are Chinese; *ki* is Japanese.

Gassho – *lit.* "palms pressed together". In the West, this would more commonly be known as "the prayer position". Palms are placed together at the heart position, at a 45-degree angle. We perform *Gassho* in Reiki when commencing a self-Reiki treatment or a session for another. We can also do *Gassho* at the beginning of meditation, and when reciting the Precepts. It is a gesture of "coming together" and of respect. It also serves to remind us (our brain) to let go of distractions, and to focus within.

Gokai – *see Precepts; Reiki Precepts*

Hara – *lit.* "belly" *or* "abdomen". It's the seat of our energy and is situated a little below the navel. It's the focus of some martial arts work, and it's our energetic centre. To breathe to the *hara* is to breathe deeply.

Hatsurei Ho – A meditation exercise within Reiki practice, handed down from Mikao Usui. Composed of three parts, this exercise helps to strengthen both our focus and our energy.

Hayashi, Chujiro – student of the founder of the system of Reiki, Mikao Usui, and master (teacher) of Hawayo Takata, who brought Reiki from Japan to the West. Originally a doctor in the Japanese Navy, Hayashi saw the benefits of Reiki and opened his own Reiki clinic in Tokyo. B. *1880* D. *1940*.

Okuden – *Japanese.* "Hidden" or "inner" teachings. The name of Reiki level two, or advanced Reiki training.

Precepts (Reiki Precepts; Gokai) – The Reiki Precepts, also known as the *Gokai*, are the written principles set down by Mikao Usui to guide us to a correct mind and state of being.

Reiju – Also known as "Attunement" or "Initiation/transmission". *Reiju* means "blessing" or "spiritual blessing", and it's the act of initiating a student into Reiki.

Reiki – The name of the energy and the system within which we use that natural or spiritual energy. It has several translations, but is usually translated as "universal life force energy", "spiritual energy" or "divine energy". It's the energy, or essence, we use for natural healing for the mind, body and spirit. The word and the system come from Japan.

Shinpiden – *Japanese*. Reiki master level, also known as Reiki level three. The word *Shinpiden* means "mysteries". It's this level where students are taught the *Reiju* and can start teaching.

Shoden – *Japanese*. Reiki level one, the first Reiki training. *Shoden* translates as "first teachings" or "beginning teachings".

Symbols – The full names of the symbols are: *Cho ku rei, Sei he ki, Hon sha ze sho nen*, and *Dai komyo*. The symbols are a part of the Reiki teachings, to help with focus and understanding.

Tanden / Dan Tien / Tan Tien – same as "*hara*" – the abdomen, the seat of *ki*, of energy within the body. Also the three tandens of *hara*, heart, and head – three energy vortices. This is a Japanese and Chinese understanding of energy.

Takata, Hawayo – Student of Chujiro Hayashi, Takata brought Reiki from Japan to the West. Takata was Japanese-American, from Hawaii. *B.1900 D.1980*

Usui, Mikao – Founder of the system of Reiki. Japanese, B.1865 D.1926. Mikao Usui was a Buddhist and founded Reiki in the later part of his life after a mountain meditation, part of his practice within his own spiritual training. He taught around 2,000 students during his lifetime, and only around 11 of these went on to *Shinpiden* training, including Chujiro Hayashi.

References

Chirico, A. et al. (2017) 'Self-Efficacy for Coping with Cancer Enhances the Effect of Reiki Treatments During the Pre-Surgery Phase of Breast Cancer Patients', *Anticancer Research*, 37(7). doi:10.21873/anticanres.11736.

Csikszentmihalyi, M. (2009) *Flow: The psychology of optimal experience*. Nachdr. New York: Harper [and] Row (Harper Perennial Modern Classics).

Ewing, J.P. (2008) *Reiki shamanism: a guide to out-of-body healing*. Findhorn, Forres, Scotland: Findhorn Press.

Fleisher, K.A. et al. (2014) 'Integrative Reiki for cancer patients: a program evaluation', *Integrative Cancer Therapies*, 13(1), pp. 62–67. doi:10.1177/1534735413503547.

Harner, M.J. (1990) *The way of the shaman*. 10th anniversary ed., 1st Harper & Row pbk. ed. San Francisco: Harper & Row.

Humphreys, K.L. et al. (2017) 'Psychopathology Following Severe Deprivation: History, Research, and Implications of the Bucharest Early Intervention Project', in Rus, A.V., Parris, S.R., and Stativa, E. (eds) *Child Maltreatment in Residential Care*. Cham: Springer International Publishing, pp. 129–148. doi:10.1007/978-3-319-57990-0_6.

Kenrick, D.T. et al. (2010) 'Renovating the Pyramid of Needs: Contemporary Extensions Built Upon Ancient Foundations', *Perspectives on Psychological Science*, 5(3), pp. 292–314. doi:10.1177/1745691610369469.

Laozi and McDonald, J.H. (2010) *Tao te Ching*. London: Arcturus.

Niebauer, C. (2019) *No self, no problem: how neuropsychology is catching up to Buddhism.* San Antonio, TX: Hierophant Publishing.

Osho (2015) *Osho: living dangerously: ordinary enlightenment for extraordinary times.* London: Watkins, an imprint of Watkins Media Limited (Watkins masters of wisdom).

Prochaska, J.O. and DiClemente, C.C. (2005) 'The transtheoretical approach', in Goldfried, M.R. and Norcross, J.C. (eds) *Handbook of psychotherapy integration.* 2nd ed. New York: Oxford University Press (Oxford series in clinical psychology).

Ricard, M. (2015) *Happiness: a guide to developing life's most important skill.* London: Atlantic Books.

Roberts-Herrick, L. and Levy, R. (2008) *Shamanic reiki: expanded ways of working with universal life force energy.* Winchester, UK; Washington, USA: O

Stiene, B. and Stine, F. (2010) *The Reiki sourcebook.* Lanham: O-Books.

Stiene, F. (2015) *The inner heart of reiki: rediscovering your true self.* Winchester, UK; Washington, USA: Ayni Books.

Weir, K. (2014) 'The lasting impact of neglect'. Monitor on Psychology, , 45(6). Available at: http://www.apa.org/monitor/2014/06/neglect.

Yamaguchi, T. and Petter, F.A. (2008) *Light On The Origins Of Reiki: a Handbook for Practicing the Original Reiki of Usui and Hayashi*

Bibliography

Reiki

Bronwen and Frans Stiene – The Reiki Sourcebook. O Books. ISBN: 978-1-84694-181-8

Frank Arjava Petter – The Original Reiki Handbook by Dr Mikao Usui. Lotus Press. ISBN: 978-0-9149-5557-3

Tadao Yamaguchi – The Light on the Origins of Reiki. Lotus Press. ISBN: 978-0-9149-5565-8

Frans Stiene – Inner Heart of Reiki. Ayni Books. ISBN: 978-1-78535-055-9

Shamanism

Llyn Roberts and Robert Levy – Shamanic Reiki. O Books. ISBN: 978-1-84694-037-8

Jim Pathfinder Ewing – Reiki Shamanism. Findhorn Press. ISBN: 978-1-84409-133-1

Michael Harner – The Way of the Shaman. Harper One. ISBN: 978-0-06-250373-2

Chris Luttichau – Calling Us Home. Head of Zeus Ltd. ISBN: 9781784979775

The mind, happiness, and meditation

Matthieu Ricard – Happiness. Atlantic Books. ISBN: 978-1-78239-481-5

H.H. Dalai Lama & H. C. Cutler – The Art of Happiness. Hodder & Stoughton. ISBN: 978-0-340-75015-5

Chris Niebauer – No Self, No Problem. Hierophant Publishing. ISBN: 978-1-938289-97-2

Amit Ray – Meditation: Insights and Inspiration. Inner Light Publishers. ISBN: 978-9382123316

Eastern Teachings

The Tao Te Ching. Arcturus Publishing Ltd. ISBN: 978-1-84837-544-4

The Dhammapada (sayings of the buddha). Penguin Books. ISBN: 978-0-14-139881-5

Osho: Living Dangerously. Watkins. ISBN: 978-1-78028-007-3

Inspirations

Julian Bound – Haiku (a book of Haiku poems). ISBN: 9781520439815

Printed in Great Britain
by Amazon